Kingdom
Moments &
Movements

Robert Glenn Johnson

Kingdom Moments & Movements

a daring how-to guide
for launching sparks of heaven

invite
PRESS

Plano, Texas

Contents

Preface

At the very young age of twenty-three, I married Linda Mitchell and we moved to Houston, Texas, to begin our life together. We joined Mt. Vernon United Methodist Church, where Jeremiah Booker began to mentor me through the ministry candidacy process. Within a few months, I started having dreams, sometimes nightmares, about this parable told by Jesus:

> At that very time there were some present who told Jesus about the Galileans whose blood Pilate had mingled with their sacrifices. He asked them, "Do you think that because these Galileans suffered in this way they were worse sinners than all other Galileans? No, I tell you, but unless you repent you will all perish as they did. Or those eighteen who were killed when the tower of Siloam fell on them—do you think that they were worse offenders than all the other people living in Jerusalem? No, I tell you, but unless you repent you will all perish just as they did."
>
> Then he told this parable: "A man had a fig tree planted in his vineyard, and he came looking for fruit on it and found none. So he said to the man working the vineyard, 'See here! For three years I have come looking for fruit on this fig tree, and still I find none. Cut it down! Why should it be wasting the soil?' He replied, 'Sir, let it alone for one more year, until I dig around it and put manure on it. If it bears fruit next year, well and good, but if not, you can cut it down.'" (Luke 13:1-9)

I would awaken from these dreams drenched in sweat and fear, and while I could never recall any details from the dreams, there were two things that would ring in my spirit: an unfruitful fig tree and sudden death.

Before the age of twenty-three, as far back as I can remember, I had always feared that I would I die an early death. So, when these dreams began, my first thought was that the same fear of death that had always been with me was still present, refusing to release its grip on my life. However, I soon began to think differently.

Because the dreams were connected to this passage, fear of death evolved into a fear of impending death tied to an unproductive life, which made a lot of sense to me, except that I didn't understand why God would bother me about living an unproductive life when, in my eyes, my life was just getting started.

By the end of that first year of marriage, however, I had more clarity. I interpreted this passage to mean that Jesus was saying that death in itself is not a tragedy, but it IS a tragedy to die without having produced anything and without having fulfilled one's purpose. God was giving me a powerful gift—the gift of learning to live with an acute awareness of the brevity of life, the call to live a productive life, and to hold these two things together in my heart. I came to believe that God was telling me, "You don't know how much time you have, so make the most of every moment, every day, every year."

Because I was given this gift, I became a person who learned to pay attention to and make the most of moments and days. I even built a playlist of songs that had that theme. I preached from this biblical passage multiple times, and it was the theme of every eulogy I did. "It's not a tragedy to die, but it is a tragedy to die without having lived the life God intended you to live, and you better get busy living it, because you don't know how long you have. You don't know when the owner of the vineyard is coming and expecting to see fruit."

People who knew me best would say they appreciated my capacity to "be fully in a moment" and to "make the most of moments."

In the early 2000s, however, I changed. I became an anxious presence. When Linda and I would visit our family in Mississippi during the holidays, my father would ask me why I seemed unable to be still. Instead of maximizing each moment, I became a person who rushed from one moment to the next.

While on vacation at Disney World in the summer of 2005, I started noticing how much my second daughter, age five at that time, had grown. As I watched her playing during various moments on that vacation, I found myself feeling surprised at some of the things she was doing. I particularly remember her being able to navigate on monkey bars with one hand. She would jog from place to place and had developed unusually muscular calves. At some point during that vacation, as I was watching her, I said to Linda, "Wow. How did I not see how Kayla has grown?" Linda replied, "You're missing it, Robert. You're not as attentive as you were with Giselle [our first daughter]. You're missing it." Of course, as we tend to do when our spouses warn us about things, I brushed it off and told Linda she was totally wrong.

A little more than a year later, in the late fall of 2006 while at the gym on Friday morning, I had a sudden onset of nausea and ran to the restroom. I remember vomiting but don't remember anything else after that except a couple of seconds of consciousness as I was being taken out of the building on a stretcher. For just a moment, I opened my eyes and saw some of the employees of the gym walking beside the paramedics and looking down at me with concern. Then I opened my eyes again, I was being placed in my car, and the nurses were giving my wife final instructions. I inquired with my wife and my friend Irv White as to the diagnosis, and they said nothing serious was found and that I had probably just had a moment of vertigo. My wife was instructed to watch me overnight, and if I had any more falls, to take me to the ER.

We went home and to the recliner in our master bedroom. My daughters gave me a bell that was sitting around the house and told me, "Dad if you need anything, just ring this bell, and we'll come to you."

The next morning, midmorning, Linda and the girls came into the room to check on me. I told them I was feeling okay and stood up to go to the restroom. Upon standing, however, I collapsed again. Linda and the girls rushed to me, got me on my feet, and somehow managed to get me to the car. I went unconscious again. When I woke, a neurologist was in the room. He said they had done an MRI since the CAT scan from the day before didn't show anything. He told me, "You've had three strokes." My mom, who had arrived with my dad from Mississippi and was a registered nurse, interrupted him and said, "You mean ministrokes or TIAs?" The neurologist responded, "No. These are full-blown strokes," as he held up a piece of paper that had a drawing of a human head with sketching he had done to show where the strokes occurred. He then said these words to me: "You all must be praying people because in all of my thirty-three years of practicing neurology, with three strokes, you have less signs of a stroke victim than I have ever seen. Now we have to figure out what caused the strokes."

After a few days, the lead neurologist entered my room with other neurologists, and they explained to me that they had not been able to pinpoint a diagnosis of what caused the strokes. They said they would keep me and keep looking.

After a few more days with me showing no other effects from the strokes except minor vertigo, they released me from the hospital with a schedule of medical appointments to continue to look for an explanation.

I left the hospital with gratitude to be alive but also gripped with fear. I was consumed with the thought, "If they don't know what caused the strokes, then they don't know how to stop them, and more strokes could happen at any time."

The next morning, my wife and daughters were about to leave for work and school and came to say goodbye. Sitting in the recliner that day, the victim of strokes of unknown causes, and not knowing if I would be alive when they returned from work and school, I hugged Linda as I had never hugged her before and did the same with my first daughter. Then Kayla, the youngest daughter, came to hug me, but I didn't just hug her. I started weeping. I grabbed her arms and absorbed how they looked. Then I pulled her closer, grabbed her face and stretched it, and began to do a fierce examination of every detail of it. Linda's words to me from the summer of 2005 came rushing back to me, "You're missing it." I stretched Kayla's eyes open and studied the size and color of her pupils. While examining her, I was praying within, "God, please don't let this be the last time I see Kayla, Giselle, and Linda. Give me more time."

The Vinedresser had come and was inspecting for fruit, and I, the guy who had once had dreams of the fig tree that was caught in unfruitfulness and had determined not to let that happen to me, had lapsed into inattentiveness.

Fast-forward a few months. My physicians concluded that although it was highly unusual, my strokes had been caused by a very small PFO (patent foramen ovale). The cardiologist who would eventually perform the surgery to address the PFO explained that due to the PFO, some blood got into the wrong place and clotted, and the clot got into my bloodstream and headed for my brain. As it traveled to my brain, however, it broke into three pieces and went to different parts of the brain. Yet, I showed fewer signs of a stroke than the neurologist had seen in thirty-three years of practicing medicine. I asked the physicians if they were sure, and they replied, "This is our best guess." I was left with my fear, and it tormented me daily, even after the heart surgery.

The resolution finally came one day when I was sitting at home, recovering from the heart surgery. Luke 13:1-9 came to my thoughts and went back to the core of my being. I realized that I was like the fig tree. I had been given the grace of "one more year" and since the physicians could only give me a "best guess" about what caused the strokes, I would have to live with the acute awareness that any day could be my last day. The gift that I had received from God in my first year of marriage came back to be stamped with an unforgettable dose of reality.

Since that time, two things give radical definition to my life:

1. I fear no one and nothing but God. I wake up every day ready to cast caution and fear to the wind in pursuit God's call and the Kingdom.

2. I try to stay attentive to life, people, opportunities, to what Jesus is doing, and to the Kingdom, and I try to make the most of each moment. This book is offered to you with that acute awareness.

I believe that the insights in this book are applicable to all people, not just Christians, so I send you into this book with a truth of which I am a witness, and it comes not from Jesus nor anyone else in the Bible. It is attributed to Buddha, but regardless of who spoke or wrote these words, I know them to be eternally true: "One moment can change a day, one day can change a life, and one life can change the world."

The Moment You've Been Waiting For

Never forget: this very moment, we can change our lives. There never was a moment, and never will be, when we are without the power to alter our destiny. —Steven Pressfield

One moment can change your life forever. It's not just a cliché. It's not an overstatement. It's not just a catchy phrase. It's true. A single moment can be an opening to a new destiny.

If we look at our current lives and ask ourselves, "How did I get here?" we'll see that we can map our lives by key moments that were turning points in our story. No one remembers every conversation, every argument, every fight, every choice, every place, or even every person he or she has experienced. We remember the highlights, and the highlights are linked to certain key moments when we, or someone in our circle of influence, made a decision that altered our trajectory or course in life. And whatever we want to change about our current lives, the first step to change is to be exposed to a moment, a "ripe" moment, a right moment, a grace-filled moment, a God-sent moment that offers us an opportunity to execute the needed action that will lead to the desired transformation.

This truth is why Martin Luther King Jr. referred to December 5, 1955, as his "day of days."[1] Four days earlier, Rosa Parks had been arrested for refusing to abide by the dehumanizing segregation laws

Chapter 1

and practices for public transportation in Montgomery, Alabama. Her action, a monumental decision in itself, ignited an organized boycott of the buses. The organizers of the boycott were hoping for 60 percent participation from Montgomery's Black citizens, but on that first day, participation was far better than they anticipated. At a meeting of the boycott's leaders and local clergy at 3:00 p.m. that same day, the Montgomery Improvement Association was created to lead and manage the newborn protest movement, and King was elected as its first president and charged with making a speech at the mass meeting that had been scheduled for 7:00 that night. By the time the meeting ended, there was only an hour remaining before the mass gathering at Holt Street Baptist Church. King usually spent several hours preparing his sermons, but that evening, he only had about twenty minutes to prepare his speech. Media outlets from across the country had come to Montgomery to cover the fledgling protest. The church was packed with an estimated five thousand people in attendance. King stood up to speak, and the rest is history.

King had just been awarded his PhD in June of that same year. The plan for his life when he arrived in Montgomery in 1954 was that he would complete his PhD, serve in Montgomery for a little while, and then move on to pastor a large church in a large city and teach in a university or seminary setting. During his speech that night, a speech that lasted approximately fifteen minutes, the Montgomery Bus Boycott became known as the beginning of the civil rights movement, and King became the movement's unofficial leader and spokesperson. His original plans for his life were dead. Everything had changed. He was twenty-six and would be dead by an assassin's bullet at age thirty-nine. By the time of his death, he had become a global icon for human rights, and it all started that night, in a fifteen minute speech. This is how a single monumental moment can change your destiny, the destinies of others, and sometimes, the destinies of hundreds, thousands, or millions of people.

It's interesting to note that King and the civil rights movement as a whole were ushered along by these big moments, these moments in which it seemed that the hand of God was invading history and bringing a little piece of the Kingdom of God into reality. These big moments kept happening until the signing of the Civil Rights Act of 1964, which, finally and completely, gave Black Americans full citizenship in the United States of America.

Ripe moments are possibilities for transformation. They are turning points and gateways to significant change, growth, or fulfillment in us, our families, our relationships, our churches, our communities, or even our cities. Living a quality and impactful life, having a flourishing family life, having a vital and transformative ministry, and getting closer to our God-given dreams and desires will be determined, mostly, by seeing and maximizing these ripe, grace-filled moments.

This perspective doesn't minimize the value of all moments. Indeed, every moment of life is a gift and a blessing for which we should remember to be grateful, but not all moments are created equal. All moments come with blessings wrapped inside of them, but not all moments are wrapped with the gifts of powerful transformation. The practice of mindfulness that's becoming more and more widespread in our culture's consciousness is helpful because it helps us pay attention to each moment, especially the moment that's right before us. However, this book is encouraging you to concentrate your attention on the "big" moments, the monumental moments that God sends us that, if attended to properly, can change destinies.

Because these moments are gateways to change, growth, and fulfillment, they are also passageways out of unrelenting misery, misery without hope, or to use a biblical term, "hell."[2] Some people stay stuck in misery because they are waiting for someone to come and save them or give them permission to be whole. Or they are hoping that the causes of their misery will just magically disappear. Or they look for ways to soften the pain of their misery so they can live with it and bear it. Or they absolve themselves of responsibility and spend their days blaming others for their misery, because for some people, it seems easier to endure misery if they see it as the result of something done to them instead of something they themselves did. It is not God's will and desire for us to live as prisoners of unending misery, and God has provided us with clear strategies for change, growth, and fulfillment.

On this very day, we will meet with God-sent moments that, if embraced, could place us on a pathway to deep transformation, deliverance from misery, healing, reconciliation, restoration, growth, or the fulfillment of our greatest God-given dreams and visions. Today could be the beginning of the turnaround we've longed for if we don't miss the moment. Are we ready to embrace and respond to the monumental moments we will meet with today?

This book is a guide to help us improve our ability to pay attention to, see, embrace, maximize, and sustain God-sent moments, not just for ourselves but also for those we love. Few things in life are as heartbreaking as watching people you love miss their God-sent moments for change and live their lives groping and groveling in misery. It's downright heartbreaking. This book offers strategies for helping ourselves, our loved ones, and our various communities get out of our misery, heal, and flourish.

The Burden of a Moment

Although it's not certain, Benjamin E. Mayes, one of Martin Luther King Jr.'s mentors, is attributed with a poem that aptly captures the power of a moment:

> I have only just a minute, Only sixty seconds in it.
>
> Forced upon me, can't refuse it.
>
> Didn't seek it, didn't choose it.

But it's up to me to use it.

I must suffer if I lose it.

Give account if I abuse it.

Just a tiny little minute,

but eternity is in it.[3]

This powerful poem captures the power of a moment. These words can be applied to every moment of life, but they take on heighted urgency when applied to the God-sent moments that can shape our destinies. The poem, succinctly and pointedly, addresses multiple dimensions of an opportune moment.

It asserts that moments are brought to us and are not something we manufactured. In Christian circles, we call this grace, which is why, above, I referred to these moments as grace moments.

The poem asserts that although we are not the creators of these moments, and although they are given to us, we DO have the responsibility to use them wisely.

The poem asserts that grace moments come with responsibility and accountability to life and, Christians would add, to God. In other words, moments are burdens that we must bear, or they will weigh us down. There's a cost when we don't live into the opportunity of a moment. We owe it to God and to ourselves to try to maximize grace-filled moments because these moments can propel us into powerful and beautiful lives. When we don't live into them, we sustain the misery of all creation (see Romans 8:18-25).

Let's be clear. We are not saviors. We can, however, help others escape misery by embracing the transforming power in God-sent moments. This has been verified in history again and again. People who have stepped into the potential and power of great moments have brought significant change, life, hope, freedom, and empowerment to masses of people.

Consider these remarkable examples:

- Martin Luther—considered to be the founder of the Protestant Reformation

- Abraham Lincoln—issued the Emancipation Proclamation

- Harriet Tubman—the most noted leader on the Underground Railroad

- Henry Ford—pioneer of fair wages and hours for workers/employees

- Susan B. Anthony—submitted the constitutional amendment for women that gave women the right to vote

- Ida B. Wells—led the fight to create anti-lynching laws in America

- George Washington—rejected the temptation to become a king in the founding of the American democracy

- Thomas Edison—inventor of the light bulb

- Marie Curie—her scientific work led to treatments for tumors

- Nelson Mandela—his self-sacrifices helped dismantle apartheid in South Africa

Each of these persons embraced a monumental moment to act in a decisive way and as a result of his or her response to the moment, MILLIONS of people were given access to better lives. Millions.

It is tempting to read such a list and think of these individuals as extraordinarily smart, insightful, creative, or innovative, but the truth is that most people who are smart, insightful, creative, or innovative never do things that change the world. What these folks have in common, more than anything else, is that they made the most of moments.

This doesn't mean that these people accomplished these things in a singular moment in time. This is not what is meant by "moment."

In this book, a "moment" is an opportunity, a doorway, a turning point encountered within a range of time, which could be a minute, a month, or even a "season" of time. Ida B. Wells didn't complete her war against lynching and lynch mobs in minutes, but over a period of years, until it became a movement that led to new laws. Her "moment" lasted for years. We can't change the world overnight. However, by "moment," we also mean the moment of decision. Although a moment can be an extended period, there is the moment in time at which we are called to make a decision.

The Emancipation Proclamation wasn't conceived and executed in a single minute of time, but there was a moment in time when Lincoln had to make a decision to issue it. Once that decision was made, the moment extended because he then had to actually carry out his decision. So, this "moment" for Lincoln extended from the time he was initially confronted by history with the need for the decision until the Proclamation was made public, executed, and enforced. *Making and carrying out a decision is how we embrace our moments, but the first step is to make a decision.*

Cornered by Destiny

God's grace and life, in general, are "big," expansive, and patient. God can have a desire or expectation for us but give us time and space to explore other options. Life can hold particular truths for a person but allow conditions to mature before forcing the issue. But sooner or later, divine demand closes in on us; we get cornered by destiny, a critical moment comes, and we have to make a big decision.

For example, this is a story that happens around us all the time. A man is born into a family with a genetic disposition to type 2 diabetes, and in his early twenties, a crucial moment comes, and life asks him to make a decision about his health. He's counseled that because of his genetic disposition to type 2 diabetes, he needs to be proactive and manage his weight and nutrition to stave off the danger. However, being young and having that sense of invincibility that young people often have, he ignores counsel, eats without discipline, doesn't exercise, and gains weight to the point of obesity. Then one day, thirty years after the initial health counsel was given, he collapses at work, is rushed to the hospital, and is eventually diagnosed with type 2 diabetes. His kidneys and vision have already been severely impacted.

While he is an individual responding to personal moments, his responses to those moments have communal impact. If he has children, his health and possible early death could have numerous negative effects on the quality of their lives. The same goes if he has a spouse. How will poor responses to these crucial moments impact his family's financial well-being? Will the expense of managing a health crisis prevent his family from contributing to help people in need in his extended family, church, community, or city? How much stress will his spouse endure because she's worried about him, the finances, and the kids? Does he have aging parents whom he will not be able to help care for because of his own health limitations? Did he have a vital business that will close prematurely because he is no longer able to run it, and how many employees will be impacted? Could his business have provided a source of wealth for his family in future generations? On and on we go in exploring the negative ramifications of his missing or failing to meet the call of crucial moments.

Now he's facing another critical moment. He's told that he must make radical changes to try to save his kidneys, his vision, and his life. Life had been expansive and patient, but now it's closing in on him and he's cornered by destiny. Now, he must make a decision, "Will you do what you have to do in order to live?"

George Washington must have been cornered by destiny to some degree when he had to decide, finally and clearly, whether he would be a king or the first president of a democracy. Abraham Lincoln, too, must have felt cornered by destiny when he could no longer put off an executive decision about slavery. Historical conditions closed in on him, and he had to decide. We could cite a thousand moments in history when the conditions of a situation pressed someone to make a crucial decision in response to a monumental moment.

The same will be true for us. We can delay decisions. We can explore other options. We can procrastinate, blame others, try to escape a call, or try to numb the pain of some kind of misery, but sooner or later, the conditions of life and the Lord will press in and press upon us, and we will have to decide.

When destiny corners you, the more people who will be impacted by your response, the more critical is the moment. This is why it is not an overstatement to refer to some moments as monumental moments. How we respond to and in these moments could affect hundreds, thousands, or millions of people, and our decisions could impact people in future generations.

I hope that this book can help us to grow wiser in our discernment and more courageous in our responses to monumental moments both as individuals and as communities.

Moments and Movements

"Wait. Isn't it widely accepted wisdom that change takes time, especially real and lasting change?" This is, certainly and consistently, what our culture tells us. We are constantly told that change, growth, and fulfillment require a process, and that we should "trust that process" and move, slowly and persistently, toward the new life we envision, patiently enduring the tedious tasks involved with achieving our desired change and growth.

I affirm and trust the processes of getting to our desired changes, growth, and fulfillment. For example, when my daughters were children, I was intentional never to get caught up in the early assessments we do to determine how smart children are. I tried to not care about that. I tried to focus, rather, on helping them develop a strong work ethic, and I took my chosen focus to the point of believing that not only did effort matter more than natural ability, but that the effort put forth in working through a process was critical to developing good character in people.

Furthermore, while I celebrate sudden, dramatic miracles of healing, I have taught in my almost three decades of ordained ministry that since most of our broken conditions develop through a long process and over a long period, that the same will be true in the healing of them. Process and time are required. Furthermore, I have taught and believed that the process of healing teaches us certain lessons that are critical for us to learn so that we don't keep landing back in the same situations. I still believe this.

So, which is true? Should we focus on "big" moments that quickly usher us into new realities, or should we just anchor ourselves in long processes and work faithfully toward our desired changes?

While these two ideas seem contradictory, they are actually complementary and represent different sides of the truth about what it takes to achieve real change, growth, and fulfillment. The difference between these two ideas is the difference between **a moment** and **a movement.** In this book, we will make and keep a careful distinction between these two ideas.

Substantive, significant, and lasting change (growth, fulfillment) often begins with a monumental *moment* and is lived out in a meaningful *movement.* Moments are the gateways into the movements through which we work our way toward fulfillment and completion of our visions and goals. Moments can feel magical while movements can feel mundane, especially if a movement wasn't launched by a powerful, inspirational moment. On the other hand, we can waste powerful moments if we don't turn them into movements of meaningful, faithful action. Monumental moments are given to motivate us into movements of measured and methodical motion. This is why both moments and movements are needed.

The reason so many of our attempts at real change fail is because we either are trying to do a movement without the magic of a moment or we are living as if we expect monumental moments to do all the work of transformation for us.

We can think of many examples of people who were stuck in undesirable situations and couldn't seem to move forward for one of the above reasons.

It is difficult to sustain a "movement" to lose weight or become a physically healthier person without being first stirred by a moment that some would call the "aha," "turning point," or "light bulb" moment. The same is true of trying to grow a marriage, deepen a relationship with children (especially adult children), pay off financial debt, sustain a savings plan, persevere in a new financial investment plan, break an addiction, develop a new habit, grow a church, rebuild a friendship, or return to school for more education. It's not wise to say that it's impossible to live out such new commitments without a monumental moment, but it is certainly very difficult.

On the other hand, we will seldom sustain the impact of big moments if we don't follow through on those moments with movement and action. We all know people who are "big moment junkies." They live their lives holding on to, searching for, and trying to create or re-create the thrill of "magical" moments, but they never move on to the kind of meaningful action that's required to turn moments into lasting change.

We will find it extremely frustrating to try to build relationships with "big moment junkies."

Haven't we heard too many stories of people who went back to being completely broke financially after having won millions of dollars in a lottery drawing? They didn't combine their monumental moment with meaningful movement.

Every pastor knows of people in his or her church who love the "high" of coming to the altar, but they never turn the power of altar moments into the practice of holiness.

Some people who call themselves advocates for justice end up being merely chasers of spotlights, a peculiar version of a big moment junkie. An injustice happens in the community. The media shows up, and the spotlight chasers, the big moment junkies, find their way to the center of the news camera. Yet, when the media leave and the social hoopla dies down, the spotlight chasers fade into silence.

In the age of social media, people can generate big-moment emotional highs when they get likes for pictures, videos, and other content they post on their social media outlets. It is important to remind them that a picture or a post is not a life. Social media stardom is no substitute for a real, meaningful, and substantive life.

Even churches can rely too much on big moments. Some churches become event-driven churches, going from high to high in the pageantry of their programs. Some churches are hooked on their exhilarating Sunday-morning worship service. Some churches are obsessed with revival church conferences.

The people who attend these churches aren't the first Jesus-followers to get lost in a big moment. On one occasion during his earthly life, Jesus went up on a mountain and was transfigured as he interacted with Moses and Elijah. Peter, James, and John were there with him, and it, no doubt, had to be an exhilarating experience for them. Peter was so awestruck that, based on the words he spoke, we could get the impression that he wanted to stay there for a while. Jesus, however, wasn't about to stay in that moment of glory. He wanted to transfer the glory of that moment into meaningful movement among the masses of people at the base of the mountain and beyond. What a powerful story with astounding implications for how we are to handle big moments (see Matthew 17:1-16).

To be clear, there's nothing inherently wrong with the passion of these churches that dwell on their preferred form of big moments. The big moments of programs, exhilarating worship services, and inspiring, uplifting revivals and conferences host unlimited possibilities for transformation, but these moments will be wasted unless such churches translate them into mission and vital ministry.

Moments and movements are like the wood types pine and oak. When I was a kid, we had a fireplace in our home, and one of my daily chores during the winter months in Mississippi was to cut, stack, and bring in firewood. My dad used only two types of wood: pine and oak. We used pine to start the fire, and then we added the oak. It was nearly impossible to have a fire at all without starting with the pine, and it was impossible to keep a newly lighted fire going without adding the oak. In the task of "fireplace management," I came to learn that if we started a fire with the pine and then added the oak, a fire that was started around 6:00 p.m. would last until deep into the night.

Monumental moments are the pine that ignite a fire, and a sustained movement is like the oak that keeps the fire going. If we allow God to ignite a good fire in our lives, and we feed it with faithful action, we can build powerful, "fired" movements that will keep on producing deep change, growth, and fulfillment, even in our "nights" (our darkest days).

A Moment in Need of a Movement, or a Movement in Need of a Moment?

A great example of how moments and movements require each other is the event considered to be the beginning of the civil rights movement: the Montgomery Bus Boycott, which resulted in the Supreme Court ruling that segregation on public buses is unconstitutional.

Under the rules of segregation on public transportation, Black people were required to sit at the back of buses, and even if they had taken a seat at the back, if a white person boarded the bus and all the seats toward the front half of the bus were filled, Black people were to give up their seats for the white person.

On that momentous day of December 1, 1955, Rosa Parks was asked to give up her seat on a bus. She refused, was arrested, and Black people in Montgomery, Alabama, launched a boycott of the Montgomery public buses that lasted for a year and removed segregation from public buses.

Some people tell the story of the boycott with an emphasis on the moment when Rosa refused to give up her seat on a bus. Sometimes the story is told as the tale of a tired little lady who was just trying to get home after a long day of work, too weary that day to cooperate with the demands of racial segregation on public transportation. Sometimes, the storyteller will say that Mrs. Parks was tired but that her fatigue gave her the courage to refuse to give up her seat. These storytellers, regardless of how they relay the story, view that moment as the spark that ignited the boycott.

Others, however, tell the story in a way that emphasizes the years-long planning and preparing that had happened long before the moment when Parks refused to give up her seat. They even point out that she had herself been deeply engaged in trainings for non-violent protest. They indicate that she was chosen by the leaders of a movement that was already in motion as the right person through whom to go public.

Both versions of the story hold part of the truth. The Montgomery Bus Boycott was a movement in need of a monumental moment, and once the monumental moment happened, it needed a movement to give it long-lasting impact. Both needs were met, and the Montgomery Bus Boycott is widely viewed as one of the most successful protest movements in American history. As a result of the success of the Montgomery Bus Boycott, Martin Luther King Jr. became one of the most influential civil right leaders in the world, but he never had as much success in future efforts as he had in Montgomery. In Albany, Georgia; Birmingham, Alabama; Selma, Alabama; Chicago, Illinois; and Memphis, Tennessee, he had limited or some measure of impact, but nothing came close to the nearly complete victory he had in Montgomery. Why? In all these other places, either the monumental moment or the methodical movement was missing. In some cases, like Chicago, Illinois, both were missing.

The closest he came again to the Montgomery level of successful protest was in Birmingham, where a protest movement had been organized and launched but was in need of a monumental moment. That "magic moment" came while King and most of the adult protesters were in jail, and because King was unable to travel and raise money for the protest, the movement was losing momentum. James Bevel, an associate of King's with the Southern Christian Leadership Conference, suggested that they involve children. When the children readily agreed, they marched, and it turned the momentum back in favor of the movement. When Bull Connor, the Birmingham commissioner of public safety, responded to the marching children with water hoses, billy clubs, and police dogs, the national media blasted the images onto televisions across the world. The tide of public opinion turned in favor the movement and in favor of giving Black Americans their full rights as citizens.

"Miracles come after a lot of hard work," writes Sue Bender.[1] However, hard work, if it is to be sustained, needs a good miracle moment, or a few, to start the work and keep it going.

Conclusion

Turning monumental moments into momentum for transformative movements is the mechanism that drives human progress. This book takes this truth seriously and will attempt to give practical guidelines for maximizing monumental moments, turning them into movements, and then sustaining those movements for lasting impact.

Before we get to the practical guidelines, let's take a look at a few stories from the Bible that show the teamwork of monumental moments and maintained movement.

Monumental Moments in the Bible

The primary idea of this book—that a single moment can change your life and destiny when it is noticed, embraced, and followed up with action (movement)—is validated in Scripture. Indeed, one way to read through the Bible is to read it as a collection of stories about *monumental moments* when the right action, right response, right words, or the right decision, at particular moments, led to success, victory, transformation, or progress for the stories' protagonists. Let's look at two well-known biblical stories to examine the wisdom they unveil about the transformative power of God-sent moments and movements.

Exodus

The liberation of the Israelites from Egyptian slavery and the ensuing establishment of independent nationhood began with a singular, powerful moment. Moses, who had been a prince of Egypt, had to flee Egypt because in an act of trying to stop an Egyptian soldier from physically abusing a Hebrew slave, he ended up killing the soldier (Exodus 2). Having effectively avoided Egyptian authority, Moses found a new home with Jethro, a priest of Midian, and his family. One day, Moses was tending Jethro's sheep and took them to the back of the wilderness, near Mount Horeb. There he noticed that a bush was on fire but was not being consumed by the fire. So, Moses decided to get closer to try to figure out if he was really seeing what he thought he was seeing. As he drew closer, Moses had a divine encounter out of which he was called and commissioned to go and lead God's people out of slavery and into Canaan.

After this powerful moment, there was a long time, a long journey, and a long list of travails and afflictions that Moses and the Israelites had to endure before they finally reached the land God promised to them. By the time they actually got to Canaan, even Moses had been disqualified from entrance into the promised land. Nevertheless, it was Moses' moment of divine encounter that God used to ignite the people's journey to liberation.

There are a few practical and powerful lessons related to the theme of this guide that we should pull from this story. A single person who has a *transforming moment* with God and has been "set afire" with God's mission can be used by God to *ignite* a "movement" that leads to change, growth, and fulfillment, in a family, a church, a business, or a community.

This is not giving a stamp of approval to our culture's unhealthy fascination with rugged individualism. Rugged individualism is un-biblical, un-Christian, and untrue. In some communities, people are growing more and more impoverished as they are trying to live by the illusion of rugged individualism.

What is true is that God created us to live in community. The Kingdom of God is essentially a community under God's reign. In spite of the negative politicization of the phrase "it takes a village," the phrase is consistent with a comprehensive, biblical worldview. It takes a village to be fully human. It takes a village to experience the fullness of God's creation. Although marriage is between two people, marriages are healthier when they are lived within community with others who support, pray for, speak life into, and help to defend the integrity of a marriage.

Nevertheless, we also know that God affirms our individuality in the context of community and that the blessing of community and the blessing of individuality are mutually beneficial. Community can enrich the lives of individuals, and individuals can in turn enrich the well-being of communities. This is true in the secular realm, but it is even truer among people of faith and people who are followers of Jesus Christ.

Moses didn't do everything that needed to be done for the Israelites' liberation, and our focus here is not to lift up individual heroism but to make us aware of God's tendency to launch great change through the simple obedience of persons who have "stood on holy ground" and have been altered by the grace of God.

Each of us who has had a deeply transformative experience of God's grace needs to stay open to the possibility that God might use us to spark a moment that sparks a movement. We should never assume such capacity out of pride, arrogance, or assumption in our human strength but humbly keep ourselves available to God to speak or live out a "movement of God" in a community or situation. So many of our families, churches, and various communities are one "Moses" away from powerful change.

It is clear that Rosa Parks, mentioned in the previous chapter, and the people who strategically chose and placed her on that bus, understood this. They didn't need her to lead the movement. We don't even know if she ever did anything else significant in the movement. She did her part. She took the fierce courage God had given her, and she positioned herself in the right place, at the right time, to be used by God to launch a movement that would help make America better. A single person, in a single moment of God-infused courage and action, helped change the world!

1. For Moses to have the moment that God used to launch the Israelites' freedom movement, he had to pay attention to God's attempt to get his attention. We are too busy to

notice the moments that God gives us. No matter how important our work is, if we are too busy to maximize a God-given moment, we are busier than God ever intended us to be.

2. We usually hear that such monumental moments are rare, but one of the biggest, surprise truths about life is *how often* we meet with such moments. In fact, they're happening all around us constantly, because this is the nature of the world God created and placed in our hands to manage, and this is the nature of the world into which Jesus launched and initiated the Kingdom of God. We live in a world that's bursting with moments that have the power to radically change our lives for the better. In the words of Elizabeth Barrett Browning, "Earth's crammed with heaven, and every common bush afire with God."[1]

A Crossroad Moment

Now let's examine the story of how the Israelites became God's chosen people, found in Genesis 11:27-12:9. Abraham's father, Terah, for some reason we are not told, gathered his family and left their homeland of Ur and set out for the land of Canaan. One of Terah's sons, named Haran, died in Ur. It's possible that Terah left Ur because he could no longer bear to live in the place that constantly reminded him of the pain of experiencing the death of a child, but no clues are given. We are also not told why Terah chose Canaan for his final destination. Nevertheless, Terah and family never got to Canaan. They got as far as Haran and settled there.

A note worth mentioning is that in Hebrew, the word *Haran* could mean "parched" or "crossroads." Either meaning gives this place, Haran, great function as a metaphor. Were the writers implying that Terah got to a place where, geographically and spiritually, he met with scarcity, despair, and persistent indecision?

20

It is not hard to imagine that Terah might have felt as if life was closing in on him, making him unable to envision a future for himself and his family. When you gather the details of his life at Haran, things were pretty bleak. His family no longer had a place to call home. In a time when social status, spiritual vitality, wealth, and power were measured by the number of offspring in one's family and the active fertility of the females in the family, Terah only had two sons, one of whom had already died, and his remaining son and his wife, of old age themselves, appeared unable to bear children. The family had come to accept the reality that Sarai (Sarah), Abraham's wife, was barren. For the leader of a sojourning family in Abraham's time and context, that's a very discouraging status and outlook.

Maybe the bleakness got to be too much for Terah, and he couldn't find the strength, hope, and vision to keep journeying on to Canaan. Whatever was the case, Terah got stuck in Haran, and finally, at the age of 205, he died, probably leaving his family in even deeper despair.

Terah's death left Abraham with the burden and weight of leading his family forward, but with all of the despair they were trying to overcome and get through, the future didn't look promising. In fact, in their context and times, Abraham and Sarai might have felt cursed.

Then comes the next chapter.

In Genesis 12:1-4, God enters the story and shows us up at the crossroads, the parched place, in a situation wrapped in indecision and despair, and offers Abraham, the leader of the desperate family, what they needed the most: the opportunity for a better life and a change of destiny. The family that no longer had a land to call home would be given a new land flourishing with fertility. The family that was diminishing in numbers would now have a family with offspring as numerous as the stars in the sky, to use the language of Genesis 26:4 where God reaffirms the promise made to Abraham in

Genesis 12:1-4. The family that had no future would be the agency to a blessed future for "all the families of the earth" (12:3).

How does this opportunity come to Abraham? As far as we can see in the biblical text, Abraham's destiny-changing opportunity comes in a singular *big moment* that requires from Abraham a singular decision to surrender to the opportunity. This moment changed the destiny of Abraham's family and all the families of the earth. Yes. It happened in a single moment!

Beyond this moment, of course, there was still work to do. Abraham and his family had to live out their surrender. They still had to face temptations to be unfaithful to God. They still had to labor, pray, and walk by faith. Big moments don't absolve us from life. Rather, they are invitations and gateways to better lives. The big moments don't permit us to skip life, which is why Abraham, as he picked up his father's journey toward Canaan, journeyed on "by stages" (12:9) continuing to make mistakes and bad decisions. No moment, no matter how big it is, will excuse us from the work of living as human beings in a broken world, and no moment, no matter how big, can ever discharge people of faith from having to walk by faith and love beyond measure.

It is also important to note that when Abraham started his journey, the first place he got to was Canaan. That meant that Terah was much closer to Canaan than he realized. It wasn't time or distance that kept him in Haran. It was the quality of the moment that could open up the future to him and catapult him into the life he left Ur to pursue.

As for Abraham, he came to realize that the life his father wanted, that he wanted too, wasn't in a particular place. That life is available anywhere, anytime, when we pay attention to and make the most of our big moments, those moments when God comes to us and invites us into a time of flourishing.

This is how the Israelites became God's chosen people. It happened when Abraham grasped the power of that moment at Haran and made the right decision to surrender to God's call.

Conclusion

The Bible is filled with inspiring examples of how God used monumental moments to bring about substantive change for the chosen people, all people, and all of creation. From this day forward, may we always remember to include the lens of "monumental moments" in our reading and interpretation of the Bible. Here are two questions to use:

1. What's the monumental moment in this passage?

2. What's the monumental moment that God is bringing to me through this passage today?

Chapter 4

Kingdom Moments and Movements

The mysterious reign of God has begun. It is full of surprises.
—Mary Catherine Nolan

The title of this book refers specifically to "KINGDOM moments and movements," because there are moments, monumental moments, and then there are Kingdom moments. To pay attention to and make the most of monumental moments is to open the door to a good life. To pay attention to and make the most of Kingdom moments is to open the door to our best life.

In 2013, I had the pleasure of going to lunch with Reverend Terry Teykl. Terry had been the founding pastor of Aldersgate United Methodist Church in College Station, Texas in the late eighties. During its early years, Aldersgate had once been one of the fastest-growing United Methodist Churches in America and grew to well over two housand active members. It was also known for being an extremely charismatic church that centered on prayer, healing, and miracles. During our lunch together, Terry told the story of how Aldersgate began and how it became a fast-growing church where lives were being transformed daily.

Terry shared that he was assigned by his conference to plant a new church, and he felt overwhelmed. So, he went into his backyard to pray, desperate for God's help. He had a seminary education and ministry experience, but he knew that he needed more. That day, in his backyard, alone and desperate, Terry prayed and asked God to "show up" and build the church. Otherwise, the work would utterly fail. What Terry was asking for was a Kingdom moment. A good moment might build a crowd, a monumental moment might build a worship center, but to transform and build people, to build a community of people who work together toward the same God-given vision, and to build a movement that would lead to the transformation of a city, Terry needed a Kingdom moment! So he determined that instead of doing what most pastors of churches do—focus on how to get people to show up for the church—he would focus on how to get GOD to show up, because only if GOD showed up could something truly powerful really happen, and if God did show up, and something truly powerful did really happen, people would show up to see what God was doing.

Missionaries who come out of Pentecostal and Charismatic traditions often say that when they go to a new city or village, the first thing they do is pray for God to show up and work a miracle, and then the revival grows from there. The miracle is the Kingdom moment that starts the fire. Then a movement breaks out that keeps the fire going. Any follower of Jesus who cares about the transformation of the world needs to have some grasp or appreciation of this idea of launching world-changing movements with Kingdom moments.

But what exactly is the Kingdom?

The core of Jesus' message, the message that is the "good news" he came to deliver to the world was this: "the Kingdom of God has come near." While he was on earth, Jesus asserted that his coming to earth was the inauguration of God's Kingdom coming to earth, and that through his followers, the Kingdom would continue to spread until the kingdoms of this world have been consumed by God's Kingdom (see Mark 1:14-15; 1 Timothy 6:15; Revelation 19:16). Furthermore, Jesus placed the highest value on the Kingdom of God, so much so that he taught us that when we pray, our main request to God should be for the Kingdom to come (Matthew 6:5-15).

The central truth that we must come to about the Kingdom is that it is not so much a place; it's a way to exist, a way of life, a quality of life, and it is a quality of life that is irrevocably connected to God, its King. Like God, this quality of life is eternal. It had no beginning, and it has no end. As human beings, we are invited by God to embrace this life, engage in it, be its witnesses, and carry it in our bosoms and beings (see John 3:16; Mark 1:14-15; Luke 9:1-6; 10:1-9). The Kingdom is not just some place believers go after we die. It is a life we can participate in and experience right now!

Now, there's another question we must ask. What are the characteristics of Kingdom life?

The best way to answer this question is to invest some time in reading through the four Gospels specifically for descriptions and characteristics of the Kingdom. This exercise in itself could provoke a godly revolution in our communities (marriage, family, church, community, businesses), especially if our community hasn't really been exposed to the full picture of the Gospels' presentation of Jesus and the Kingdom. (For a more comprehensive exploration of Jesus and the Kingdom, see my book, *Jesus Unchained*.)[1]

However, we need to give attention to a few *critical characteristics of the Kingdom*. In the Gospels, through the life of Jesus, we can see that the Kingdom life defined in several ways:

- surprising and life-exchanging experiences of God's love, toward us, among us, and through us (Luke 15; Matthew 5:38-48; 8:1-3; 9:1-7; 9:35-38; 11:25-30; Luke 7:36-50; 13:10-17; John 3:16)
- expansion of God's will on earth, marked by miracles of healing, provision, and faith (Mark 5:21-43; 7:31-37; 8:1-10; Matthew 14; Luke 10:1-20; John 5:1-15)

26

- defeat of the kingdom of darkness and demonic forces, marked by sounds and sights of anguish as they are confronted by Jesus and the will of God (Mark 1:21-28; 5:1-20; Luke 9:37-42; Matthew 8:28-34)
- self-sacrificing service, including how power is used and employed (Matthew 25:31-46; Mark 10:35-45; Luke 10:25-37; John 13:1-17)
- reversal or dismissal of dehumanizing social and religious rules, roles, and divisions (Matthew 4:18-22; 5-7; 8:5-13; 9:8-13; 12:1-14; 15:21-28; Luke 1-2; 7:36-50; 8:1-3; 10:25-37; 12:13-21; 13:10-17; 14:15-24; 17:11-19; 18:15-17; 19:1-10)
- a higher moral and ethical standard based on the love of God functioning in human hearts (Matthew 5-7)

If the Kingdom is a life that God offers to us now, and we are to embrace this life, pray for it, live it, bear witness to it, and help to spread it, then followers of Jesus are people who look for **moments** when:

- we are given access or deeper access to Kingdom life

- we have an opportunity to bear witness or bear greater witness to the Kingdom, or

- through us, the Kingdom is able to make a deep or deeper invasion into a community

Let's look quickly at examples of each of these types of Kingdom moments.

A Woman Battling an Illness Is Given Access to Kingdom Life

A woman had been losing blood for twelve years. In desperation, she had spent all of her money seeing doctors, but instead of her condition improving, it worsened. One day, she got word that Jesus was passing through her village, so she gathered herself and made her walk over to the road where she knew he would pass. Although Jesus was surrounded by a large crowd and it would be extremely difficult to get to him for help, the ailing woman determined that no matter what it required of her, she was going to do all she could to give herself a chance to get to Jesus and get the healing she needed. "If I can touch the hem of his garment, I know I will be made whole," she said to herself (Matthew 9:21 paraphrased). She discerned that it was her moment, maybe her last-chance moment, to save her own life. As it turned out, she was right. It was a moment for her, a Kingdom moment. She placed herself at the right place, at the right time, and took the right action, all in faith, and a door opened that gave her access to Kingdom life (Matthew 9:18-22; Mark 5:27-28; Luke 8:42-48).

Jesus' Disciples Are Given an Opportunity to Bear Extraordinary Witness to the Kingdom

After hearing that his cousin, John the Baptist, had been executed, Jesus attempted to withdraw and be alone, but when the people of the nearby areas found out where he was, they went to him, and Jesus compassionately ministered to them. When the evening came, Jesus' disciples came to him, and when they saw the crowds of people, numbering over five thousand, they advised him to send the crowds home where they could find food and rest. However, Jesus had a different perspective. He saw this as an opportunity, a moment in which the disciples could engage in a profound act of service that would bear witness to the Kingdom. So, Jesus said to them, "They need not go away; you give them something to eat" (Matthew 14:16). Jesus then took the lead in this witness-bearing moment, and with only five loaves of bread and two fish, he and the disciples miraculously fed the crowd. Afterward, the disciples took up twelve baskets of leftovers. What the disciples had initially interpreted as a problem on the brink of becoming a disaster became a moment in which extraordinary witness was given to and about the Kingdom of God (Matthew 14:13-21).

Jesus Sends a Kingdom-Possessed Man Home to Spark a Kingdom Invasion

A man had been possessed with so many demons that when he met Jesus and inquired about his name, he responded, "My name is Legion, for we are many" (Mark 5:9). Jesus cast the demons out of him, and upon his next public appearance, the man was radically changed. Instead of living as a naked, wild man in a graveyard, he was "sitting there, clothed and in his right mind" (5:15). As Jesus was departing the area, the man begged Jesus to allow him to become one of his disciples, but Jesus told him, "Go home to your friends, and tell them what great things the Lord has done for you, and how He has had compassion on you" (5:19, NKJV). Jesus perceived an opportunity, a moment for a Kingdom invasion of a community. If this man went back among those who had known and given up on him because of his demon-possessed life, through his very presence, he could lead a Kingdom-invasion in his community (5:1-20).

Conclusion

Let's rehearse this: followers of Jesus are people who look for **moments** when:

1.   we are given access or deeper access to Kingdom life

2.   we have an opportunity to bear witness or bear greater witness to the Kingdom, or

3.   through us, the Kingdom is able to make a deep or deeper invasion into a community

Can you identify recent experiences of one of these Kingdom moments in your personal life, your family, a relationship, your church, your workplace, your community, or your city?

Now let's explore how can we better discern and make the most of the Kingdom moments that come to us.

Chapter 5

How to Discern a Kingdom Moment

The world is full of miracles that most of us never see. We have not trained ourselves to look. —John Killinger

Sometimes, it is crystal clear that we are in a monumental moment. For example, when a young woman receives a marriage proposal, she's obviously in a monumental moment that has the power to shape the rest of her life and her destiny. The same can be said of the player in an NCAA March Madness Tournament game who gets called on to take the last shot of a game to determine whether his or her team will win or lose. That one shot will determine the direction of millions of dollars and the future of a university's basketball program.

By the way, isn't it interesting how some people seem to have a knack for missing big moments while some seem to have a flair for mastering big moments? Have you ever wondered what makes them different? We'll come back to this question later in this book.

For followers of Jesus, too, there are times when we know that a Kingdom moment is before us. For example, when the Word of God is duly preached or taught and people are invited to respond in some way, that's an obvious Kingdom moment. Such a moment is jam-packed with destiny-shaping implications for the persons invited to respond and even for their children's children.

Another example of an obvious Kingdom moment is when a church receives an unexpected, large, financial gift. How that church receives such a gift and responds can have generational impact for good or bad.

John Wesley's "Aldersgate moment" in which he had a decisive experience with the Holy Spirit was a Kingdom moment, much like Paul's encounter with God on the Damascus Road (Acts 9:1-30). The impacts of both moments are still being experienced throughout the world to this very day!

When a miracle happens, that is an obvious Kingdom moment. It is important that we learn to see every miracle as a gateway into the Kingdom. It is an explicit invitation to draw closer to God, to enter the Kingdom, to expand our experience of the Kingdom, and to expand our understanding of the Kingdom.

Whenever we encounter moments in which the character attributes of the Kingdom, known also as the fruits of the Holy Spirit, are being displayed, we are, of course, experiencing a Kingdom moment. *Whenever we see or act with humility, repentance, forgiveness, faith, patience, kindness, extravagant generosity, joy, peace, self-discipline, self-sacrificing service, and self-sacrificing love, we are in moments that can be utilized to further expand our experience of God's reign* (see Galatians 5:22-23; 1 Corinthians 13; Matthew 5-7; Matthew 22:36-40; Matthew 25:31-46).

We also find obvious Kingdom moments in everyday life: getting an unexpected financial blessing; surviving a deadly accident or health event; a child inviting a parent to have a conversation that the parent has been desperately waiting to have; a friend asking for help or counsel; a coworker asking for prayer; a major life transition; or even a major crisis. We'll examine more later about how major crises are always Kingdom moments.

But what do we do when Kingdom moments are not as obvious? What are some signs and indicators that we are encountering a

Kingdom moment that's just not as obvious as others? What are the pockets of our lives where Kingdom moments are present just beneath our normal gaze?

Less-Obvious Signs and Locations of the Kingdom

1. Unplanned Community

Essentially, the Kingdom is a community, a community under the reign of God. Furthermore, according to what Jesus told us through a prayer he taught his disciples, God is reigning wherever God's will is done (see Matthew 6:10). Wherever God's will is being done amidst, by, and through a gathering of people, we are experiencing a portion of God's Kingdom. Matthew 18:19-20, says, "Again, truly I tell you, if two of you agree on earth about anything you ask, it will be done for you by my Father in heaven. For where two or three are gathered in my name, I am there among them." When we encounter a moment in which we witness people working or living together in a way that they are fulfilling some part of God's will, we know we are encountering a Kingdom moment.

For example, in my work as a pastor, I have often had the experience of finding out that a group of people in the church had gotten together and started engaging in some kind of service that had not been planned by church leaders or put on the church's calendar. Yet, it was obvious that the group of people was doing God's will. Many church leaders and pastors would stop such activity out of need to make sure that they are in control or because they view such random activity as people operating in disunity. I learned over the years to see it as the random work of the Holy Spirit, and to see my job, and the church's, as figuring out how to cultivate and support what the Holy Spirit was doing. This understanding is not meant to encourage the random splintering of ministry in local churches. Rather, it is a reminder that God is always busy in ways among us that we did not plan and cannot control. Sometimes, rather than creating our own ministry agendas, we need to look around and see what God's up to and join in!

Beyond the local church, where are you seeing people working together to fulfill some aspect of God's will?

It is important to acknowledge with this sign that there are times when knowing God's will in a situation is not as clear as other times and requires that we engage in more prayer and discernment.

Also, people don't have to be intentionally seeking to do God's will to be engaged in a Kingdom moment. In such cases, Christ is present in their deeds, and even if they are not doing God's will with intention, followers of Jesus can still discern the "Kingdom-ness" of the moment and maximize it.

2. Visible and Audible Irritation of Evil Powers and Presences

Very early in Jesus' earthly ministry, there was a time when he was in Capernaum on a Sabbath day. He went into the local synagogue to teach, and out of nowhere, without any verbal or physical provocation from Jesus, a demon-possessed man had voices come out of him that said, "Hey! Leave us alone! Jesus the victorious, I know who you are. You're God's Holy One and you have come to destroy us!" (Mark 1:21-25, TPT). This is one of the most revealing stories in all of the Gospels and New Testament. It unveils a clash between the kingdom of evil and the Kingdom that Jesus came to launch. Even if the human beings in the synagogue that day didn't fully recognize the fullness of Jesus' identity and mission, the demons did, and they clearly realized that by his presence and mission, Jesus was dismantling, disabling, and subduing them.

This same dynamic happens for followers of Jesus wherever we go, without the kind of direct confrontation with evil presences that happens with "deliverance ministries" in some Christian Charismatic and Pentecostal circles. Followers of Jesus don't have to directly confront supernatural evil. It is disturbed by our very presence. It is disturbed by the presence of the Holy Spirit within and upon us.

The presence of Jesus-followers not only disturbs the supernatural realm of evil; it disturbs the natural realm. For example, I think, often of the evil that was aroused whenever Martin Luther King Jr. or any other segment of the civil rights movement entered a city. Every time King entered a city, from St. Augustine, Florida to the last city he visited, Memphis, Tennessee, the individuals, systems, and structures that were vehemently opposed to integration and/or full citizenship for Black Americans demonstrated extreme irritation, hate, and violence. King's very presence, even as a voice of nonviolence and love, stirred up the most intense evil in people who were committed to a segregated society.

As parents know so well, sometimes raising a question with a child can arouse extreme volatility and erratic behavior. This is not to say that those children are evil of course, but that they may be under the influence of negative energies that don't want to be disturbed, called out, or confronted. The same kind of response can be experienced when raising a simple question and making a simple suggestion to a spouse, a coworker, a friend, a boss, a business partner, and especially, a religious leader. The same response can be experienced when we engage with the powers that be in a community, city, or nation. Many churches located in economically challenged communities have frightening testimonies of confrontations with gangs in those communities, not because they directly confronted those gangs but simply because the gangs perceived their presence as threatening.

Can you recall times when you witnessed that your simple presence, question, or suggestion seemed to provoke irrational, volatile, or even violent responses?

When these kinds of incidents happen to and around us, they can be startling and intimidating, but we need to recognize that the irritation is a sign that the Kingdom of God is showing up in some

35

way, and we have a moment in which we can cultivate and expand the Kingdom of God among us.

3. When Encountering Strangers and Strangeness

It is a normal tendency to see the Kingdom among people, places, and activities that are familiar and beloved to us. Furthermore, we tend to be more readily discerning of the Kingdom when it comes to people we like and people of whom we want to think and believe the best. For example, most parents seem to be supernaturally gifted at seeing goodness, talent, and the hand of God at work in their own children. On the other hand, we often miss Kingdom moments when they show through people we don't know well or who have ways of living, thinking, and believing that are different from our own. This is so true that after knowing someone for a while, we will sometimes assess that the person has improved or grown spiritually, when what really happened is that we learned to appreciate his or her differences. We grew in being able to see God at work in the individual's life.

Sometimes, God sends blessings into our lives wrapped in the packaging of strangers. This is why the writer of Hebrews tells us, "Do not neglect to show hospitality to strangers, for by doing that some have entertained angels without knowing it" (13:2). (By the way, this divine counsel is given right after the writer counsels his readers to let love continue within their Christian fellowship. This is healthy to remember because sometimes churches and believers behave as if practicing hospitality with strangers cancels out love of those in the body of Christ.)

Jesus himself was actually a stranger to many of the people he encountered and blessed during his ministry on earth. In the life of Jesus, there are several stories in which people to whom Jesus was a stranger perceived that God was at work in him, and although they were not people who would have explicitly embraced the Kingdom that Jesus was bringing, their perception of God's presence and their willingness to lean into it, led to miraculously wonderful results for them. Examples are the hemorrhaging woman in Luke 8:40-56, (there is debate about whether she was a Jew or a Gentile. For an in-depth investigation of this debate, see an article by David Shaw in the *Bulletin for Biblical Research*),[1] the Roman soldier in Matthew 8:5-13; and the Syrophoenician woman in Mark 7:24-31 and Matthew 15:21-28.

In the case of the latter, the Syrophoenician woman, Jesus emphasizes the fact that they are strangers to each other by telling her that he came to help his own people, not strangers: "It is not fair to take the children's food and throw it to the dogs" (Matthew 15:26), he says to her. Yet, by her uncanny perception of a monumental moment with the divine, she pushed through words to which she might have taken offense, and by so doing, she experiences the miraculous healing of her daughter, as Jesus says to her, "Woman, great is your faith! Let it be done for you as you wish" (15:28).

Local churches miss some of their most opportune Kingdom moments because we have a tendency to discount, disdain, and disallow strangers, whether they be strange to us by lifestyle, appearance, belief system, verbal accent, race, style of worship, preference of Bible translation, or religious affiliation, and contrary to popular opinion, this tendency is not restricted to the older generation. Young adults can be just as dismissive of people because of something, such as, a clerical garment, a hairstyle, or a tattoo. The mistake we're all making is assuming that God can't be active in someone who is different from us, and by making such assumptions, we end up missing many Kingdom moments.

In my work as a pastor, I have made it a habit to look for the strangers around the churches I serve with the expectation that they are connected to a God moment of some sort. In my years of engaging in this practice, I have never been disappointed. I have learned that when strangers show up in your church or life, there's usually some divine purpose at work. Because strangers don't "fit in" with our lives and communities, getting to know them and trying to discern how God is using them to bring Kingdom transformation can often be difficult. In many cases, they don't "speak our language" or share our cultural values. We are tempted to turn away from them and turn back to the people who are like us. However, we must guard against this temptation because we know that the God we serve has a penchant for showing up to us through strangers. If we neglect to be hospitable with strangers, we are choosing to opt out of untold numbers of Kingdom opportunities.

Local churches can be just as dismissive of strange activities. Anyone who's been active in a local church long enough has heard the theme statement of many local churches: "We've never done that before" or the alternate version, "We've never done it that way before." How many of our churches are mired in dysfunction because of the dogged refusal to look for God's presence in strange approaches, strategies, and methods for ministry, worship, and fellowship?

If we compare such a way of thinking to the full biblical witness, it should make us squirm. Over and over again, the biblical narrative of God's redeeming, repairing, and restoring of creation is advanced by God being at work through people and ways that were considered strange. We need look no further than the story of how God became a human being: a virgin birth through a common couple! As Mary says of herself, "My soul magnifies the Lord, and my spirit rejoices in God my Savior, for he has looked with favor on the lowly state of his servant" (Luke 1:46-48).

Furthermore, followers of Jesus understand how Kingdom moments can be hidden in strangers and strangeness because we ourselves are called and commanded, literally, to be different. In the Methodist/Wesleyan circles, we refer to this as sanctification, which means that God's grace is making us different from the rest of the world. The writer in 1 Peter 2:11 reminds Christ's followers that we "are like visitors and strangers in this world. So I beg you to keep your lives free from the evil things you want to do, those desires that fight against your true selves" (ERV).

In Acts 1:8, Jesus tells the apostles, "But you will receive power when the Holy Spirit has come upon you, and you will be my witnesses in Jerusalem, in all Judea and Samaria, and to the ends of the earth." Most of the places listed by Jesus are places where they will be encountered as strangers. Fortunately, in all of the places where the apostles went to bear witness to the Kingdom, they encountered people who saw God at work in their strangeness. That's how the Kingdom spread and the church grew.

In a recent reflection on this matter of how following Jesus can turn us into strangers, I surmised that the deeper we get into our divine purpose, the less we and our purpose will be understood by our family and friends. This was true even for Jesus. His family never understood his purpose, and although the at-large crowds embraced him at the beginning of his ministry, by the time he got to the cross, his tribe had dwindled down to two people: one of his disciples and his mom. This is how it works. Divine purpose will eventually make us strangers to family, friends, and followers. So, if you're following God's directions for your life, and your recent maneuvers have confused your crowds, that could be a very strong signal that you've landed smack dab at the center God's will.

The call to see the Kingdom in strangers and strangeness is why there is great power and potential in the Fresh Expressions movement. It is encouraging local churches to be exceptionally attentive to the people, ways of life, and ways of gathering that lie outside of what is normal or familiar to us. The mission statement on the website of Fresh Expressions United Methodist reads, "We cultivate communities of love and grace for people neglected by the church.

The four values of these new faith communities are inclusive, accessible, transformative, and connectional."[2]

It is very important to note that we can also encounter divine strangeness in ordinary life. In all the places where we work, play, and do life, God is as much at work in much of what is strange as in what is familiar. Kingdom moments are awaiting us in unfamiliar people and unfamiliar places, packed with possibilities for transformation. Identify the strange places and people in your life, and at least once a week, go on a Kingdom adventure to explore how God might be waiting to surprise you.

Questions for Reflection

Who are the strangers God has sent into your life? What are some of the strange activities that God is using to bring the Kingdom near to you? Do you have stories of times when a stranger entered your life, family, community, or church and ended up proving to be a tremendous blessing and expansion of the Kingdom for you?

4. Activated Enemies

Closely related to encountering Kingdom moments in strangers and strange activities, we often encounter the Kingdom through people we view as enemies. Is this not part of the significance of the story of the good Samaritan told by Jesus in Luke 10:25-37? The Samaritan who stops to help the wounded man is the hero of a story Jesus tells a group of Jewish leaders. It is commonly known that during the time of Jesus, Jews hated Samaritans. Their hatred of these "half-breed Jews" had been cemented into their thinking and common practices. For Jesus to use a Samaritan as the hero of this story is to imply that divine activity can happen in the very people whom the Jews viewed as enemies of God and God's people.

When we have moments when our enemies seem to be activated, those are Kingdom moments. In these moments are opportunities to build understanding; to practice the love ethic of Jesus, which has transforming power; and practice forgiveness, humility, patience, trust, and courage. Almost nothing impacts how people view followers of Jesus more than observing how we handle conflict. This is not to say that Kingdom moments caused by activated enemies will lead to reconciliation with your enemies. Like all Kingdom moments, we seldom fully know all that God is planning and working, and God can do far more in such moments than just reconciling us with our enemies. At minimum, we ourselves will grow in our faith and love of God. Loving and serving our enemies can mature us in immeasurable ways.

While giving his first exposition on the Kingdom, it is not incidental that Jesus included this instruction:

> "You have heard that it was said, 'You shall love your neighbor and hate your enemy.' But I say to you: Love your enemies and pray for those who persecute you, so that you may be children of your Father in heaven, for he makes his sun rise on the evil and on the good and sends rain on the righteous and on the unrighteous. For if you love those who love you, what reward do you have? Do not even the tax collectors do the same? And if you greet only your brothers and sisters, what more are you doing than others? Do not even the gentiles do the same? Be perfect, therefore, as your heavenly Father is perfect." (Matthew 5:43-48)

Jesus is calling us to "exploit" activated-enemy-moments with radical love so the Kingdom may be expanded in our own heart. Wow!

5. Problems

A problem is merely an opportunity for something good to happen. We don't need to live our lives with the illusion that a great life is a life without problems. Rather, we should see our series of problems as a pathway to an expanded experience of the Kingdom life.

This is why Jesus was constantly taking his disciples into places and situations where they were confronted with problems. It was almost as if Jesus were saying, "My followers are problem solvers, and the only way to learn how to solve problems in the Kingdom way is to practice solving problems in the Kingdom way." So, off they went, from facing a storm to facing a demon to facing mass hunger, on and on, one problem after another. Jesus knows that problem-solvers are peacemakers, pathfinders, pioneers, and playmakers for the Kingdom!

Chapter 14 in the Gospel of Matthew is a powerful example of the intensity of Jesus' program of developing his disciples to be problem solvers. The chapter begins with them being informed that John the Baptist has been executed. Next, they are faced with the problem of feeding five thousand people in a deserted area. Before the last bites of fish in the miraculous mass meal were finished, Jesus was beckoning his disciples into a boat to cross back over to the other side of the Sea of Galilee, and according to Matthew, he has to force them into the boat. Why? Their hesitation may have been caused by their last crossing of the Sea of Galilee. On that trip, they thought they were going to die, and now, Jesus was wanting to go back across the lake. As soon as they reached the other shore, they ran into more problems. Crowds were waiting to be ministered to.

In chapter 15, more problems, including another challenge to feed thousands of people. In both cases of the feeding miracles, the disciples seemed to want to get rid of the problems, not solve them (Matthew 14:15-17; 15:32-33). They wanted to pass the problems on to others, which is what people tend to do in life. Jesus, however, doesn't ignore problems and leave them to be someone else's headaches. He solves problems and teaches those who follow him to be problem solvers, as well.

It is worth a moment of reflection to consider the example of Jesus in light of these words from the great late psychiatrist M. Scott Peck:

> Life is a series of problems. Do we want to moan about them or solve them? Do we want to teach our children to solve them? . . .

It is in this whole process of meeting and solving problems that life has its meaning. Problems are the cutting edge that distinguishes between success and failure. Problems call forth our courage and our wisdom; indeed, they create our courage and our wisdom. It is only because of problems that we grow mentally and spiritually. When we desire to encourage the growth of the human spirit, we challenge and encourage the human capacity to solve problems, just as in school we deliberately set problems for our children to solve. It is through the pain of confronting and resolving problems that we learn. . . .

This tendency to avoid problems and the emotional suffering inherent in them is the primary basis of all human mental illness.[3]

You don't have to agree with Peck, his ideas, or even the proposed findings in the general field of psychiatry to appreciate what Peck suggests here when lined up alongside how Jesus mentored and trained his disciples.

Even with life in general, is it not true that the greatest people and greatest accomplishments came from solving great problems?

- Abraham Lincoln led the effort to solve the problems of slavery and a civil war, and this is why many historians rate him as America's greatest president ever.

- Jackie Robinson stepped forward to help solve the problem of segregation in professional baseball. He remains, to this day, one of the most respected athletes in in the history of American sports.

- Martin Luther, the great catalyst of the Protestant Reformation, was trying to solve the problem of the widespread manipulation and abuse in the Catholic Church.

- Mother Teresa became a great figure in history because she was trying to solve the problem of a lack of care for the poorest of the poor in Calcutta.

- Sojourner Truth has lasting influence in American history because she was trying to solve the problems of racial and gender inequalities.

43

- John Wesley became the great founder of the Method-ist/Weslyan Movement because of his desire to solve the problem of needed reform in the Anglican Church.

But we aren't limited to famous people or celebrities to see how problems can become invitations to greatness. Make a list of the top ten people who have had the greatest impact on your life and identify what problem they helped you to solve.

Encouraging followers of Jesus to move toward problems and become problem solvers can unsettle some believers because they will be cautious that we are encouraging a "salvation by works" instead of "salvation by God's grace alone" theology. However, solving problems is not attempting to save ourselves. We trust in God alone for our salvation, and we fully embrace that we are saved only by God's grace and not our works. Yet, we know also that God's grace isn't limited to our personal salvation. The grace of God pervades all of life, and the grace of God is more than mercy and forgiveness. God's grace gifts us with the capacity to do God's will and solve problems.

As Kingdom dwellers, we don't ignore, hide from, or pass on our problems. We face them with confidence in God's grace. We know that every problem presents us with the possibility of a Kingdom moment.

Let's learn to apply this bit of wisdom from the late General Colin Powell to ourselves as followers of Jesus and as local churches: "Leadership is solving problems. The day soldiers stop bringing you their problems is the day you have stopped leading them. They have either lost confidence that you can help or concluded you do not care. Either case is a failure of leadership."[4]

Now, here's a rewrite of that statement with some adjustments: Following Jesus is, in part, about solving problems. The day your loved ones, friends, and the community stop bringing you their problems is the day you have stopped influencing them for Jesus and the Kingdom. They have either lost confidence that you can help or concluded you do not care.

6. In Conflict

One of the major problems we have as human beings is working through conflict, whether it is interpersonal or between groups of people. Because most people, including followers of Jesus, don't know how to work through conflict in a healthy way, conflict is packed with opportunities to create or cultivate Kingdom moments. In working through conflict, we will have multiple opportunities to employ the "keys" of the Kingdom, such as patience, kindness, speaking the truth in love, tenderness, endurance, strength, courage, forgiveness, hope, and faith, and whenever we employ some of the "keys" of the Kingdom, we are inviting and cultivating the Kingdom in our midst.

On the other hand, we miss the Kingdom movements and Kingdom moments when we constantly avoid conflict. By avoiding conflict, we do the reverse of creating and cultivating the Kingdom. We end up creating cracks, crevices, and crannies where the kingdom of darkness can hide, breed, and grow without confrontation. For example, many parents know the experience of avoiding a conflict conversation with a child about some kind of unhealthy behavior. By the time they finally decide to have the confrontation, which was probably by force, the darkness has deepened, strengthened, and matured. Because the conflict was avoided for far too long, what was originally a problem that could have been addressed with guidance, therapy, or soft management toward corrective behavior ended up being a severe problem that required major intervention. This is what can happen when we avoid conflict. We don't just miss the Kingdom. We give covering and protection to evil.

Leaning into conflict invites the Kingdom to come in and transform, enrich, deepen, and mature our relationships.

Leaning into conflict doesn't mean, however, that we are always engaging in confrontation. Sometimes we lean in by praying, by researching and preparing for the conflict, or by waiting attentively for a Kingdom moment that opens the door to confrontation and challenging conversation. One Kingdom moment can lead to the next until a Kingdom movement is happening.

When we address conflict on the social level, beyond interpersonal relationships, especially as related to politics, it is even more important that we don't think that working through conflict is always about confrontation. It is more important that we understand that when working through conflict, we need more than just the right information or the right argument. We also need the right moment.

When Jesus launched the Kingdom, he told his audience that he was the right person with the *right message* about the *right blessing* and with the *right instructions* for how to receive the blessing. He also said it was the *right time*! (See Mark 1:14-15.)

Anyone who has done social justice work long enough has learned that timing is as important as the message and the messaging. A protest march or a boycott has no power in itself. It has to be done at the right time.

In interpersonal or social conflict, how do we know when it's the right time? We'll know because it will be at a moment when people's hearts and minds are open and vulnerable to conversation, change, or listening. Of course, such a moment is in itself a Kingdom moment that is linking us to the next Kingdom moment of working through the conflict. Sometimes it takes a first Kingdom moment to get to a deeper Kingdom moment. A God-timed moment is a great opportunity to turn a destiny.

To be clear, it is entirely possible to engage in the work of addressing social conflict at any time, but for followers of Jesus, there is a certain outcome that we are looking for that requires divine timing. Working through social conflict can be done through agitation, protest, advocacy, or revolution; but our goal, as followers of Jesus, is Kingdom transformation, and Kingdom transformation is possible only when we merge the right message, the right messaging, the right messengers, and the right methods with the right moment.

It is also important to note that conflict resolution that gives way to Kingdom transformation is not about changing others. It's about changing how we relate to each other. If we give any attention to people changing, we should focus on allowing God to change us. This is how God works among us. Every time we go to God asking God to change "them," God changes us first and experiencing more of God's transforming grace becomes another reason why conflict can be a gateway for a powerful Kingdom experience.

7. Fear

Fear keeps us from a thousand blessings and opportunities, and every day, people miss moments because there's something frightening attached to the moment. I refer to these frightening attachments as spiritual "scarecrows" that Satan puts in place to frighten us away from the wonderful things God has planned and designed for us.

Because of our faith in God, followers of Jesus are not turned away by Satan's scarecrows. We face and confront things that initially frighten us because we remember that the "scarecrow" means that there are opportune moments, great potential, and tremendous opportunities near!

This different approach to fear has been built into the spiritual DNA of the leadership team at Resurrection Church (United Methodist), a megachurch with six campuses in the Kansas City metropolis. Consider this leadership principle that they share with leaders, shared with me by Dan Entwistle, who serves as Resurrection's managing executive director:

Another leadership principle I want to share with you is discernment by nausea. We have learned that whenever there is an important decision to make and there are two paths before us, the way we almost always know which path is the right one to pick is the one that make us sick to our stomachs and makes us toss and turn all night.

We learned this early. When we were meeting in the funeral home and had outgrown it, there came an opportunity to meet in two possible buildings. One was a little church that would take us from 90 seats to 150 seats, and it had stained-glass. It was nestled in a beautiful neighborhood, but there would be no room to grow. But, it had nurseries, and a small parking lot, and it would mean no more set up and tear down. Ahhhhh!

The other alternative was to go to an elementary school gym where we would have to set up folding metal chairs, put up a banner system to cover the large leopard mascot on the wall, and we'd have to arrive at 6 in the morning on Sunday mornings to set everything up for church. And we couldn't store anything there.

We would have to work hard to make this school gym look and feel like a church or we could have our own church building with stained glass windows and permanent nurseries. So, leopard or stained glass?

Which one of those do you think felt better? Our entire leadership team at that time was like, "Let's get that church! How cool would that be to have a place with stained glass windows?"

And then we remembered—discernment by nausea. Setting up at the school every weekend felt hard—it made us sick to our stomachs to think about it, but as we prayed, we knew it was the way we were supposed to go.

You do not decide to do the hard thing without a leader who can inspire and motivate people to make sacrifices to remind them of their purpose. That one decision made all the difference.

Where would Church of the Resurrection be today had we chosen to meet in the church with no parking and no visibility because it was hidden back in a residential area, as opposed to choosing to meet in the elementary school?

So, those crossroads happen all the time. There's a thousand different times we made decisions when it was the hard decision, and it was always the right decision.

"Discernment by nausea!" What a great example of how followers of Jesus turn fear on its head to see what opportunities lie beneath it.

8. Outside the Rules.

One of the absolutely great things about God is how God comes to the rescue of people who have gotten or fallen outside the rules. In this case, the rules referred to aren't God's rules. Rather, they are the rules of society and organized religion. More than half to most of Jesus' miracle-blessings and words of affirmation were for people who were outside of the rules of ethnicity, social status, or religious condition. The Syrophoenician woman was of wrong ethnicity (Mark 7:24-30). Zacchaeus, a tax collector, was of the wrong social and religious status (Luke 19:1-10). The woman who washed Jesus' feet with her hair was of the wrong religious status (Luke 7:36-50). One of the main accusations that Jewish leaders made against Jesus was that he was a friend of sinners and tax collectors (Matthew 11:19), and Jesus did "rule-breaking" things, such as healing on the Sabbath (Mark 3:1-6; Luke 13:10-17), touching lepers (Matthew 8:2-3), and telling people that their sins were forgiven (Matthew 9:1-8). Jesus told stories that imply a kind of favoritism toward people who, supposedly, live outside the rules.

- A son disrespects his father and leaves home full of arrogance, but on his journey back home after failing miserably at life, his father breaks the rules, runs to meet him, and gives him a welcome inappropriate for a son who has gotten outside of the rules.

- A sheep wanders off from the herd and away from the watch of its shepherd, but when the shepherd realizes that the sheep is missing, he leaves the entire herd to find the one lost sheep who has wandered outside of the rules.

- A coin gets dropped accidentally and falls outside the realm of lighted visibility, but the coin's owner searches in the darkness until she finds the lost coin. (This is also, by the way, a powerful story with widespread and penetrating implications about where we might find God at work, creating Kingdom moments.)

Families, churches, communities, and movements can get fractured and begin to decline while simultaneously disaffiliating themselves from people who have gotten outside the rules, not realizing that it's the disaffiliations that are killing us and that new life from God is to be found by exploring divine possibilities among the "outsiders."

A pointed example of this came to me when a foster care advocate came to meet with me about supporting the agency for which he worked. He said he had been meeting with lots of pastors, but most of them seemed uninterested. He said to me, "These pastors tell me that they are desperate to reach children and youth, but what they want are enfranchised kids from two-parent households living the American dream. They don't want kids from foster care, with missing parents and with mental and emotional problems, because if they did, I could give them more youth and children than they could dream of handling. There are plenty of kids who would die to have the love, attention, and support of a church family!"

This man's words came home for me at Saint Mark United Methodist Church. While the church was still doing virtual services, I got a message from a youth in my church whom I had not met saying, "Pastor Johnson, please reopen the church. We need to come together." As I inquired about the sender of this message, I discovered that she and her brother were living in a foster home and that she was battling brain cancer. Gradually, we reopened our doors, and on Easter Sunday 2022, this beautiful girl stood on the stage and danced with the church's dance team. In all my years in the church and as a pastor, I have never seen the kind of joy and purpose on a volunteer's face as I saw on Sophia's.

One day, while scrolling on a social media platform, I noticed a picture of her brother, Johan. He was on a truck that was decorated to participate in a parade. All on his own, he had decided to put his drum set on the bed of a truck and participate in a parade in their hometown, which is about forty-five minutes north of Wichita, Kansas. The truck and the drum set were covered in decorations that read, "Saint Mark United Methodist Church." Johan proudly and joyfully represented his church in a parade in his hometown!

To this very day, Sophia and Johan are participating in Saint Mark's Youth Ministry and are joyfully engaged every week in some form of Kingdom service. Sophia and Johan, by no choice of their own, live outside the rules of traditional life and traditional family, but the people of Saint Mark will testify that in Sophia and Johan they encountered a once-in-a-lifetime KINGDOM MOMENT.

Oftentimes, we teach the Christian life as if it's about knowing all the rules and successfully abiding by them and then having a wonderful life if this is accomplished. But what about the people who have fallen outside the rules? What about the people for whom the rules won't work because their lives are too broken? What about the people who tried the rules and failed miserably? Have you yourself ever felt that you had fallen beyond the reach of the rules and needed a miracle?

The good news is that God extends extravagant love to outsiders. And when God's people want to know where God is at work in the world, we have to start looking more among the people who are outside of our rules.

Even in our personal relationships, this truth can help us. All of us have some part of ourselves that's hanging outside the norms. We can help and love one another better when we learn to look for God in and be of service to the outsider dimension of each other.

9. In Failure

Throughout the Bible, we are told of instances in which God used failure as turning points towards the Kingdom. We understand this because we know that we are exceptionally humble and vulnerable when we feel we have failed.

This is not to say that there's something inherently magical about failure. Failure breaks a lot of people to the point of no return. Sometimes, however, failure becomes a turning point and people launch from failure into an exceptional life.

Think of the story of Michael Jordan. Thousands upon thousands of high school kids have been cut from their basketball team, and most never bounded back. But Michael Jordan turned such failure into motivation and momentum to become arguably the greatest basketball player of all time.

If you were to do a Google search of "people who succeeded after failing," you would be astonished. The fact of the matter is that most of the people who have succeeded wildly succeeded after, and in many cases because of, profound failure.

For example, "Before she became the star of daytime TV, Oprah Winfrey was fired from her job as an evening news reporter at Baltimore's WJZ-TV because she was 'unfit for television news and couldn't sever her emotions from her stories.'[5] Yes. This is THAT Oprah, the media mogul who is now a billionaire!

The precept that failure can be a gateway to greatness is even truer in the Kingdom. Before we fail, we are often too arrogant, prideful, and stubborn for God to use. When we fail, our hearts become vulnerable, our spirits are broken and penetrable, and our minds are open to new learning. It is when we are in such a state of brokenness and openness that God can get through to us, and when God gets through to us, miracles of life, service, impact, and achievement tend to happen.

When Peter stood on the day of Pentecost and preached the first sermon of the newborn church, and three thousand souls were saved, is there any doubt that this Peter was created by the profound failure of betraying Jesus in Jesus' moment of greatest need of the disciples' support (see Acts 2)?

This truth about life and the Kingdom gets added weight and dimension when the failure is public. It's one thing to fail. It's an entirely different and heavier thing to fail publicly. Yet, public failure can be a saving grace.

Part of the reason we often miss the saving grace and don't change after our failures is that we are so good at hiding our failures from public view. As a matter of fact, so much of social media is manipulation of the public images of people who have failed. People have come to believe that regardless of their failure, what matters most is if they can create and sustain a narrative and image of success on social media. This kind of deceit and manipulation is a disease for our souls and turns common failure into something far darker, that is, fraudulence and fakeness.

A prominent pastor I know once got exposed on video, engaging in an immoral act. The church he led and the city in which he lived were shocked and devastated. I remember feeling hurt and embarrassment for him and expressed my feelings to another pastor friend of mine. His words to me that day are unforgettable. He said, "As bad as this is, and as embarrassing as it is for this pastor, this experience could be his moment of saving grace because now that he has been exposed and is on the brink of losing everything, he's humble, contrite, and vulnerable to God in a new way, and he has the chance to come clean, live without secrets, and finally align his life with God's Word. So, although he's broken now, thirty years from now, he may look back at this moment as his greatest moment of freedom and deliverance. Instead of feeling sorry for him, I feel sorry for all the pastors and church leaders who haven't been exposed and will continue to live in disobedience to God's Word and will. As they hide in their failure, they may gain the world and lose their souls." What a monumental grasp of Kingdom truth.

In our own lives, in our families, in our churches and communities, in our cities and nation, where's the failure? It's painful to face our failures, but in them are sparks of heaven waiting to be fueled and ignited for Kingdom moments.

10. In Suffering

One thing that frightens us away from Kingdom moments is the threat of suffering. Many people have decided that no opportunity and no great moment is worth the risk of suffering. Followers of Jesus, however, learn to view suffering differently.

We know this: we will all endure our share of suffering. We will not all suffer in the same ways, but we will all suffer, and we will spend a great deal of our lives enduring and trying to understand the meaning of our suffering. Another lens for reading the Bible is to read it as a series of stories, experiences, and reflections on how human beings deal with suffering in relation to our connection with God.

There are innumerable conclusions in trying to understand the reasons and meanings of suffering, but here's what we all know to be true: suffering has tremendous transforming power, and this is not incidental.

Most followers of Jesus would agree that the greatest moment in history was made up of two events: Jesus' death and Jesus' resurrection. This means that the moment that brought the greatest transformation and blessing to the world was steeped in an experience of profound suffering. Jesus suffered an excruciating death, but we believe that through his suffering and death, "God was in Christ reconciling the world to Himself" (2 Corinthians 5:19 NKJV).

In the Revelation of John, there's a little meaning-packed nugget of insight connected to Jesus' death that's worth our attention and deeper reflection. In Revelation 5:12, in regard to the "Lamb who was slain"(NKJV), most Christians have interpreted this to be a reference to the crucifixion of Jesus, but later in John's Revelation, Revelation 13:8, more information is given. It is said that the Lamb was slain "from the foundation of the world" (NKJV). Without getting in too deep of an interpretation of these words, we can at least conclude that they imply that the slaying of the Lamb is a reality built into the very essence of the world. Could it be that suffering is an embedded and necessary aspect of life?

However, we don't need to understand the cosmic importance of suffering to know its potential power to transform us. We've seen suffering transform people into some of the most joyful, grateful, wise, resilient, courageous, faith-filled, and loving people we know. As they battled cancer, endured deep grief after the unexpected death of a loved one, braved betrayal by a friend or family member, dealt with a divorce, fought their way back from financial disaster, or tried to pull away from abuse, just to name a few of the kinds of suffering we see and experience, these people were transformed and became sources of light and hope to others. Let's make a list of such people we know and keep that list in the place in our home or office where we pray, because our prayers should be influenced by the examples of these magnificent souls. It is no wonder that these words of Ernest Hemingway resonate with us so deeply: "The world breaks everyone and afterward many are strong at the broken places."[6]

Why does suffering seem to produce such power and beauty in human souls? Perhaps it is because suffering opens us up and makes us vulnerable to bigger truths and to God. Suffering has the capacity to give us limitless numbers of Kingdom moments. People who open their souls to God when they are enduring suffering not only experience exponential spiritual growth themselves, but they can become living resources of wisdom and inspiration for others.

Derek Amato has savant syndrome. In 2006 at the age of thirty-nine, Derek suffered a head injury but survived. One day, while recovering, he got out of his bed, sat at a piano, and although he had no education or training on the instrument, he began to play as if he had been practicing all his life. A horrible accident had turned him into a musical savant.[7]

Savant syndrome is not unique to Derek Amato. It occurs frequently. One out of ten people with autism are savants. We don't want to minimize the suffering of people with autism and their loved ones who care for them, but maybe, just maybe, savant syndrome is an extreme sign of how God can turn tragedies and suffering into human brilliance, especially when we, followers of Jesus Christ, choose to open our souls to God as we suffer and seek to see the Kingdom moments born from our suffering. The thought is worth some reflection.

Of course, none of us wants to get into the "suffering line" to access Kingdom moments. We would be foolish to ask for or pursue suffering. We can be sure that a dose of it is coming our way if we aren't already in the midst of a round of it.

And we need not fear suffering. Whatever we go through, God is with us, and if we open our souls to God, we will meet with a multitude of surprise blessings that are Kingdom moments and opportunities to let the Kingdom take up greater space in our souls and our lives.

Conclusion

Every moment of life is not an explicit Kingdom moment, but every moment of life has the potential to be embraced and utilized as a Kingdom moment. Every moment of life comes to us with the potential to transform us. Some moments seem bigger or more powerful than others, but how we perceive each moment says more about us than it does the moment. Hopefully and prayerfully, this book is helping to equip us to better maximize more of our moments, individually and collectively.

In order to be better equipped, we need to consider what causes us to miss moments and how we can avoid missing them.

Chapter 6

Missing Moments

People in that robotic, drone-like state, walking the earth with no set mission other than to survive another day. Missing the glory of the day, missing the potential for beauty and magic that each moment brings. Missing the gift of life, to walk in the footsteps of the mundane.
—Tony Curl

Do you have any regrets about missed moments? Which regrets stick out more than others for you? Do you understand how you missed these moments? If you could have those moments again, what would you do differently? All of us could make a long list of missed moments in our:

- marriages
- relationships with our children, parents, siblings, relative, and friends
- careers
- management of our health
- financial management
- new life adventures
- opportunities to participate in social change that ended up being on the right side of history
- opportunities to grow closer to Jesus and grow in our faith

- serve others and make a difference in their lives

- witness to others about Jesus and the Kingdom

- model the Kingdom life in a way that would draw others to Jesus and the Kingdom

Eighty-five-year-old Nadine Stair movingly captured the sense of regret about missed moments in a poem she wrote that became popular in the late 1990s.

> If I had my life to live over, I'd dare to make more mistakes next time.
>
> . . .
>
> Just moments, one after another, instead of living so many years ahead of each day.[1]

The R and B group Boyz II Men, has a song entitled "Water Runs Dry," which was a global hit in the late 1990s. It describes a dynamic in many romantic relationships of people taking each other for granted, missing moments until the relationship completely falls apart:

> Let's not wait till the water runs dry
> We might watch our whole lives pass us by[2]

"Water Runs Dry" is not only a beautiful song but one of the most important and meaningful songs and artistic contributions in American history. Although it refers specifically to a romantic relationship, its wisdom is applicable to *all* relationships. God is speaking to those who listen to this song a message that we all need to hear. People often miss moments and wait until it's too late to appreciate life and loved ones.

You can probably name a few of your favorite songs that give the same message of being careful in life to not miss our moments, especially our moments in relationships. It would be a spiritually nurturing experience to create a playlist of such songs and spend a couple of hours listening to them, reflecting and recommitting yourself to the spiritual discipline of seizing important moments and opportunities.

We miss moments as groups as well. Married couples, families, communities, and cities, and even nations can have regrets about missed moments. We are being warned that we will, at some point soon, have global regret about missed opportunities to repair our environment on the planet unless we make drastic changes to how we interact with it.

Many African Americans share some sentiments of regret about missed moments in our history. Could we have managed and done more with the magnificence of the Harlem Renaissance? In our struggle for integration, did we give up the internal community wealth, excellence, and nurturing that had developed in some predominantly Black neighborhoods? Have we at times placed too much hope in the kindness and generosity of others instead of cultivating our own resources and capacities?

Do we, as Americans, not have many collective regrets about moments we missed as a nation that could have made our country better, stronger, and more unified?

Churches could make long lists of missing moments to

- impact their community
- appreciate good leadership
- welcome new members
- embrace the next generation
- better manage finances
- partner with communities organizations for good work
- partner with other churches

- participate in a citywide activity that could have enlarged their influence in the city

- appreciate a member who died unexpectedly

What moments has your family missed? How long would the list be of moments missed by your family, church, or community?

We are often told not to have regrets, and while there is indeed some wisdom to this counsel, we should also recognize the importance of taking time to reflect back on our lives and acknowledge missed moments and missed opportunities. In doing such reflection, we do not need to fall into despair and wallow in regret. That is not the point of such reflection. Rather, the goal in looking back is to learn, and from the grief of missed moments, we can actually find added motivation to get better at paying attention in the future. We can't go back and change the past, but more moments are coming, and we can prepare ourselves to be ready to make the most of them.

Jesus had a lot to say during his ministry on earth about missing important moments, something that he seemed to view as having tragic dimensions. He displayed regret and grief over people missing their big moments.

- In a parable, a fig tree is caught unprepared for a moment of accountability (Luke 13:6-9).

- A rich man misses his moment to follow the Lord of life (Mark 10:17-31).

- In a parable, a rich man misses life because he's busy building bigger barns (Luke 12:13-21).

- In a parable, five bridesmaids were unprepared for the arrival of the bridegroom and missed their big moment (Matthew 25:1-3).

- A man who had been lame for thirty eight-years and had positioned himself by a pool of healing water had missed so many moments that Jesus wondered if he really wanted to be healed (John 5:1-4).

- Jesus weeps over his nation because they missed their God-moment (Matthew 23:37-39; Luke 19:41-44).

Let's pause and reflect on our most painful experiences of missed moments. If we need to, let's even give ourselves a moment to grieve, and then let's move on to explore how we can have fewer of these regrettable experiences. And let's not forget to pause, reflect, regret, and grieve collectively, as couples, families, and churches.

Churches should have an annual day to reflect on missed moments from the past year, mourn, repent, and recommit. Engaging in this spiritual discipline would prove enriching to faith communities on multiple levels.

In America, at a time in which we are deeply divided, a national day of reflection would be immeasurably healing. Such a day would invite us as a nation to engage in the actions of *acknowledging* missed moments from our past, and *grieving, repenting,* and *recommitting* ourselves to building a better democracy.

For all of us, in various ways, after we reflect, grieve, and repent, then we must move on to changing our response to opportune moments. So, we need to answer this question: "What can we do to stop missing so many of our moments?"

First, we need to better understand what causes us to miss moments, and then we need to get a grasp of what is required to seize and maximize moments.

Let's take a look at some of the reasons we miss moments. Each one is worthy of further discussion:

- We didn't recognize the moment for what it was.
- We were too busy to notice what was before us.
- We noticed the moment but got distracted by other cares.

- An addiction kept us from embracing the moment.
- Idolatry caused us to reject the moment.
- We were not prepared, not equipped for the moment.
- The moment was too big for us and overwhelmed us mentally, emotionally, and/or spiritually.
- We fumbled or mishandled the moment.
- We procrastinated in responding to the moment.
- We felt obligated to self-identity, people, places, things, or a tradition.
- We didn't like the packaging in which the moment came to us.
- We lacked the faith required to seize the moment.
- We felt that we couldn't embrace a moment because of fear that it would expose secret sin.

There are probably other reasons people miss Kingdom moments, but this list above is expansive. Take some time to see if you can identify other reasons not included in this list. Also, do an exercise in which you recall some of your most-regrettable missed moments and see if you can identify the reason you missed them.

Conclusion

Here's a sobering final reflection: no matter how much we try not to, we will miss some big and some divine moments in life. Missing such moments is unfortunate, sad, regrettable, and sometimes tragic, but we are still alive and God is gracious, and although we can't get missed moments back, we can find encouragement in this irrefutable fact: more divine moments are coming, and if we pay attention and make the most of them, they will lead us into more of the abundant life.

One final thought: there will be many times in life when people will miss the moment that we offered them or that God offered them through us. This reality is poignantly expressed in a quote I've seen often on social media: "Sometimes, you love people in a language they cannot understand." When people miss the moment that we give to them, it can feel like rejection to us, and as a result, we can find ourselves harboring hurt and resentment, rejecting people in return, and misapplying Scriptures, such as "Do not give what is holy to dogs, and do not throw your pearls before swine, or they will trample them under foot and turn and maul you" (Matthew 7:6), or, "If anyone will not welcome you or listen to your words, shake off the dust from your feet as you leave that house or town. Truly I tell you, it will be more tolerable for the land of Sodom and Gomorrah on the day of judgment than for that town" (Matthew 10:14-15). While there are times for sure when these verses can be applicable to our experiences of people rejecting our efforts to serve and love them, we shouldn't rush to apply these words or use them to spiritualize our feelings of rejection and vindictiveness every time people don't embrace our gifts.

It is sad to see people walk away from their spouses, children, families, churches, and God-purposed jobs because they misinterpret people's failure to embrace the gifts the one leaving offered. There's a better and more godly way to respond.

Instead of responding with anger, vindictiveness, and reverse re-jection, we should seek to be as gracious toward people as God is toward us. Most people don't wake up each day thinking, "Just to irritate the Lord, I'm going to try my best to miss as many moments as I possibly can." Likewise, when people fail to see or appreciate the gifts we offer to them, it's not because they get up each day of their lives with the intent to reject or dismiss us. As is true with us when we miss the moments God sends us, people are doing the best they can to make sense of life and figure out how to make life work. So, let's not take these disappointments as personal attacks. Let's forgive, and let's stay open for the next moment God gives us to be a blessing for the people who "missed" us the last time.

Let's turn now to explore a spiritual regimen that can help us to miss fewer moments and make the most of more!

Chapter 7

A Spiritual Regimen for Making the Most of Our Moments

Pay attention. We miss so much of life, beauty, love, and purpose because we live our lives with an attention deficiency. We pride ourselves on being able to multitask, but we end up getting less done and missing the important stuff that's right before our eyes, minds, and hearts. If we are missing life in general because we are too busy, we will most definitely miss the opportune moments coming our way. Kingdom moments typically do not come in a loud or extrusive way. Except when they come through some kind of crisis, they come to us through the ordinariness of life.

I have found the words of Rabbi Lawrence Kushner on this topic to be particularly helpful and encouraging:

> Perhaps the burning bush wasn't a miracle but a test. God wanted to find out if Moses could see mystery in something as ordinary as a bush on fire. In order to see it as a miracle, Moses had to watch the flames long enough to realize that the branches were not being consumed and that something awesome was happening. Once God saw that Moses could pay attention, God spoke to him. Much later, when God was ready to give Moses the Torah on Mount Sinai, God said, "Come up to Me on the mountain and be there" (Exodus 24:12). Rabbi Menahem Mendl Morgenstern, from the town of Kotzk in Poland (whom we call the Kotzker Rebbe), asked: "If God told Moses to come up on the mountain, then why did God

also say, 'be there'? Where else would he be?" The answer, suggests the Kotzker, is that not only did God want Moses to be up on the mountain, God also wanted him to pay close attention, to be fully present. Otherwise Moses would not really be there. Often people are physically in a place, but because they are not paying attention they might as well be somewhere else.

Judaism has a unique way of remembering to pay attention. It is called a *berachah*, or a blessing. It begins, *Baruch atah Adonai*, "Holy One of blessing," *Elohenu melech ha'olam*, "Your presence fills creation." Then we add words appropriate for the occasion, like "who brings forth bread from the earth," or "who removes sleep from my eyes and slumber from my eyelids," or "who spreads the shelter of peace over us."

Each time Jews recite a blessing, they are effectively saying, "Pay attention. Something awesome is happening all around us."[1]

I hear in the rabbi's words some helpful guidance for growing our capacity to pay attention. We need to be present. Pay attention and engage fully with what is right before us. Look for revelation.

This will, of course, be harder for some of us than for others. Wherever we are on the attention spectrum, we can start there. Practice paying attention for five minutes, then thirty, then an hour. We will go in and out of attentiveness, but that is okay, as long as we are being intentional about continuing to practice. Soon we will start seeing amazing things all around us that were always there but had evaded our attention, and it will seem as if the world and people are coming alive when the only thing coming alive is our attention and appreciation of life. If we can keep practicing this, we will start to notice that it seems as if God is speaking to us a lot more than ever before. Because we know that we have been practicing the discipline of paying attention, we will know that it's not that God who is speaking more but we who are listening more.

Embrace the moment. When we pay attention, we will notice more Kingdom moments, and when we see them, our next step is to embrace them. This means that we name the moment, define it, and

67

consciously acknowledge that it is being given to us as a gift from God.

To name and define it means that we identify what the moment is calling us to do and what the moment will lead to.

At this point in the process of making the most of a moment, we don't need to make any public claims or professions. We are naming, defining, and acknowledging for ourselves what the moment is offering us.

Naming, defining, and acknowledging a Kingdom moment requires faith, because we will be tempted to play it safe and tell ourselves things like, "This might be a moment," "I'm not sure," "We'll see what happens," "I'll wait for further confirmation," or "If it's meant to be, it'll be, so no need for me to take any drastic actions." There are times when these statements are highly appropriate, but not when God is offering you a Kingdom moment. Using them to respond to a Kingdom moment is go to the brink of mishandling a moment. And while there is nothing wrong with waiting for clarity, we will never have enough information to take away the risk of faith.

Embracing a moment by faith means acknowledging to ourselves, although we may not use these exact words,: *"This is a Kingdom moment, an offer from God for me [or us] to experience _____, and as I [we] embrace this moment, it will allow me [us] to experience more of God's Kingdom!"*

Embracing and acknowledging a Kingdom moment may seem simple, since it is primarily a mental exercise. However, it is no small task. As we all know, the greatest battle, often, to beginning a Kingdom journey, is having the confidence and faith to admit that such a moment is indeed a Kingdom moment. We have to believe that God is at work in a moment and believe it enough to act on it.

Submit to the moment. Once we have embraced a moment by faith, we must submit to the moment, meaning that we yield to and come under the authority of the action that the moment requires of us.

For example, suppose a dad wants to grow closer to his toddler. One day, circumstances cause him to be at home for an entire day alone with just his daughter. They have eight to ten hours of time to spend together. A faith-filled father will pay attention, see this as a Kingdom moment, embrace the moment, and then submit to a day of activities with his daughter in faith that Kingdom blessings will eventually unfold.

The actions taken in submission to a moment will have to be actions of faith, because we will not have enough information to guarantee that we are taking the right action or that our actions will produce certain results. As followers of Jesus, we walk by faith and not by sight (2 Corinthians 5:7). We know that whatever is not of faith is missing the mark of God's will for us (Romans 14:23), and that without faith it is impossible to please God (Hebrews 11:6). So, there is no way to embrace a Kingdom moment without taking a risk or without exercising faith.

In Luke 17:12-19, we read a marvelous story that demonstrates the need to embrace Kingdom moments in faith. A colony of lepers encountered Jesus as he was passing through on his way to Jerusalem. Hoping that Jesus would heal them, they cried out, "Jesus, Master, have mercy on us!" When they caught his attention, Jesus ordered them, "Go and show yourselves to the priests." This was the protocol for lepers who thought they had been healed of leprosy. They were to go to the priests and have them confirm the healing before they could fully reenter society (Leviticus 14:3-7). Notice that Jesus doesn't heal them and then tell them to go. He says, "Go," and as they went, they were healed. The action of these lepers is exactly what is needed to embrace a Kingdom moment. They embraced the moment with clarity for what it was, what it would lead to, and how they needed to respond to it, and then they acted in faith. It was only after they acted in faith that the desired healing manifested.

So it must be with us when we meet a moment. We have to submit to the needed steps of faith. Only then will we begin to see the full unfolding of the blessing tucked into the moment.

Surrender to the moment. After submitting and experiencing the initial unfolding of the blessing in a Kingdom moment, then we are ready to turn the moment into a "movement" of sustained action and ongoing reality. We do this by fully surrendering ourselves to the actions demanded by the moment. People can submit to a moment for a moment, but if we want the moment to become our new reality, we have to "come out with our hands up" in surrender and commit ourselves to repeating the required behavior until it leads us to the future we desire.

Using our analogy of the dad and daughter above, surrendering would require the dad to be intentional about planning more days with his daughter. Rather than just a onetime submission to a dad-and-daughter day engagement, having dad-and-daughter days could become a regular routine. It is then that he will begin to see growth in his relationship with his daughter.

Let's consider a few more examples.

There are people who submit to an hour of intense prayer at their church's prayer vigil, and then there are people who have surrendered to a regimen of daily intense prayer, and the difference will be clear if you ever ask these two people to pray for you in the middle of a crisis.

There are people who submit to God once or twice a month during a Sunday morning worship service, and then there are people who have surrendered themselves to live for God every day of their lives, and the difference between these two persons will be unveiled in their giving, their faithfulness, their countenance, and their service.

There are marriages in which people submit to each other on special occasions, such as birthdays, holidays, vacations, or family gatherings, and then there are couples who are surrendered to the discipline of engaging in acts of service and love toward each other every day, and there is a profound difference between these two types of marriages.

There's a difference between a leader who occasionally submits to putting the organization's needs above his or her own and the leader who has surrendered to such behavior and lives it out within the organization on day-to-day basis.

There's a difference between a social justice organization submitting to the demands of activism and advocacy when there's been a major crisis in the community and the media's cameras are everywhere and the organization that has surrendered to the work of activism and advocacy every day, in the moments and places after the spotlights and possibilities for "fifteen minutes of fame" are gone.

To turn Kingdom moments into Kingdom movements, we have to surrender to sustained action that leads to our preferred reality. Otherwise, we will mishandle our moments, and our moments will never lead to real change.

Conclusion

Encountering a Kingdom moment can be a very powerful and overwhelming experience, so much so that we are ever tempted to grasp the moment, hold on to it too long, and turn it into an idol. It will help us to know that as great as the Kingdom moment is, the greater miracle is what it can turn into and become if we manage it well. Furthermore, by responding to and properly managing Kingdom moments, we can become God's partners in building miracle lives. As wonderful as a miracle moment is, it's better to live a miracle life.

From now on, when you meet with a Kingdom moment, may God also give you the grace to be phenomenal in how you respond to the moment![2]

Let's end this chapter with this affirmation: *faith-filled and faithful responses to God's grace in Kingdom moments transform our lives into magnificent movements of Kingdom life.*

Chapter 8

Cultivating Kingdom Moments

God is the giver of Kingdom moments. Kingdom moments are gifts that flow out of the heart of God through the grace (unmerited favor) of God.

Sometimes we deceive ourselves and begin to think that we have earned certain moments and opportunities with our ability to "get it right," and conversely, that when others don't get the same moments, it's because they failed to live up to God's standards enough to deserve these moments (as if we ourselves did). Let's get rid of such self-righteousness. We can certainly cultivate the favor God gives us, but we can never be good enough, productive enough, hardworking enough, or righteous enough to earn God's favor.

Furthermore, while some of us feel a bit deserving of opportune moments, the truth of the matter is that even better moments are coming to people whom we would judge, on a human level, to be far worse and far less deserving. If the most self-righteous among us had any idea how many astonishing moments God is offering to people who are considered the "scum of the earth," we would be vulnerable to a mental breakdown. That's how good God is to all of us! The reason we don't see how amazingly good God is to "bad" people is that they are probably neglecting their moments.

So, let's stop judging people for what we assume they aren't getting, and let's stop thinking that we are earning our blessings of

73

Kingdom moments. We are just as reliant on God's grace as everyone else. *We cannot create Kingdom moments.* We receive the moments that God gives us.

We can, however, *cultivate* Kingdom moments!

First, let's become fully conscious of this truth: *Kingdom moments are gifts from God, which place upon us a burden of responsibility and productivity.* Jesus' parable of the talents in Matthew 25:14-30 clearly says that there is accountability for the gifts God gives us and that, to some degree, future rewards will be given according to how we use the gifts we have already been given. So, the gifts God gives us and the Kingdom moments God gives us can be cultivated and expanded if we manage them wisely. How do we do this? Let's explore three ways we can cultivate Kingdom moments.

Prayer

Noticing and maximizing Kingdom moments requires, as you know by now, spiritual discernment, which can be defined as the capacity to see life, people, situations, and the world as God sees them. While there are many ways to develop our discernment, including study of the Word of God, fellowship with wise and mature believers, personal experience, and worship, PRAYER may be the most direct way because of what prayer actually is.

We are familiar with the "ACTS" understanding of prayer:

- A: *Adoration* of God

- C: *Confession* of our sins to God

- T: *Thanksgiving* unto God

- S: *Supplication* to God

We are also familiar with thinking of prayer as *intercession* and *petition.*

When we participate in prayer vigils or prayer gatherings in local churches and beyond, most of the time is usually spent in one of these forms of prayer.

But in a very basic sense, prayer is communication, which means we should talk to God and **listen** to God. Most prayers prayed by people, including many Christians, are monologues, not dialogues, and if we are honest, we would admit that they are more like soliloquies (talking to oneself) than monologues. Prayer is communication. *The highest form of prayer is listening for what God wants to say!* When was the last time you participated in a prayer gathering in which most of the time was spent listening to God? Could this be why the church of today, in spite of all of our financial, technological, intellectual, educational, social, and even political resources, is rapidly and increasingly fracturing and losing influence? Could our lack of listening to God be the real reason we can't seem to make disciples for Jesus Christ who don't define themselves more by their political affiliation than by their commitment to Jesus Christ? Could our lack of listening to God be the reason we seem powerless in the face of growing evil in all facets of our churches, families, communities, and societies? Could it be that we miss so many monumental Kingdom moments because as a result of not listening to God, we lack the discernment necessary to see them?

Of course, there are clear reasons why we don't listen to God: we are arrogant, and in spite of how much we sing of giving ourselves away to God, we want to be in control of everything that concerns us. We want to be in control not just of ourselves but of our spouses, our children, our siblings, and our friends. We want to be in control of our churches, our schools, our communities, and our nation. We want to rule the world. Our way of praying has become a witness to the true state of our hearts. When we pray in arrogance, we pray so that we feel in control. We do all the talking, we set the agenda, we determine the priorities, we give God a task list, and to top it all off, some of us feel the need to be super repetitive, super loud, and super emotional. as if God is lethargic, lazy, attention-deficient, or needs to be motivated or inspired to act.

While we are ordering the universe, we are missing Kingdom moments because we aren't listening for what God wants to say to us and show us.

Just to note, there are a gazillion theological holes and problems in this way of praying that this book isn't purposed to address, but let's at least acknowledge a big truth here. The problem with the world isn't God's action or inaction, but ours, and the ultimate purpose of prayer isn't to get God to do something but to get us to do something. This is not to say that God doesn't respond to intercession petition with gracious actions and blessings, but the ultimate victory in prayer is when God's people are activated to live God's will on earth as it is in heaven! Sometimes, in response to prayer, God changes things, but the ultimate change is when God changes us and we turn our conversations with God into faithful and joyful obedience to God's Word and will. The greatest goal of prayer is not trying to get God to think our thoughts but to receive God's words inside of us, so much so that they will be like "fire inside our bones" (see Jeremiah 20:9).

When we have listened and have inhaled the words of God, they shape how we see everything, and we will have a supernatural capacity to notice when God is up to something BIG in our world.

It would be worth our time to do a survey of the biblical story to see how many times big moments happened and were rightly discerned after people had been in a time of prayer.

Prayer helps us discern a moment. Prayer helps to know how to properly respond to a moment. Prayer helps us know how to nurture and extend a moment. Prayer gives us access to God's mind about how God wants to manage God's moments and the movements that grow out of them. These are the reasons why prayer is so powerful, and this is how we can best discern and manage the God moments sent to our families, our children, our churches, our schools, our communities, our movements, our nations and our world!

Evangelism

For the sake of the journey that we are on in this book, consider this broader understanding of evangelism. View evangelism not just as inviting and guiding people to a moment of spiritual salvation. View evangelism as inviting and guiding people to the next big decision or change that God wants them to make! A father may need to be evangelized back to his family. A wife may need to be evangelized back to her husband. A city may need to be evangelized to serving its most vulnerable citizens. A church may need to be evangelized to more praying or to more corporate worship. A person may need to be evangelized to his or her true calling. Broadening our understanding of evangelism in this way doesn't minimize the urgency of essential evangelism, because in all of the examples above, people's rejection of or wandering away from particular things is tied to the wandering of their souls away from God and God's will for their lives.

Surrendering or returning to God or God's will for us doesn't happen in one moment. There are smaller, *preparation moments* that prepare the way for and eventually give way to the big moments when a pivotal decision is made. This is how it happened for each one of us. We didn't "get saved" in a single moment, although we like to tell such stories. All of our lives, through every person and every experience, including our worst experiences, the Holy Spirit has been at work trying to win our hearts to God.

Evangelism, in our broader understanding of it, cultivates Kingdom moments because it can be used by the Holy Spirit to do the work of leading people to the big moments of decision, or it can be used by the Holy Spirit to help with the work of guiding people toward the moment of decision.

Notice that this way of understanding evangelism assumes that the Holy Spirit is already at work in people's lives before we arrive. We don't bring God to people. Wherever we go and among whomever we go, the Holy Spirit is already working, using a variety of ways to move people toward God, their Creator, Sustainer, Provider, Redeemer, and Judge.

Prayer helps evangelism in cultivating moments because through prayer we can better know when the Holy Spirit is using us to nudge, guide, pull, and push versus when the Holy Spirit wants to use us to bring the person or persons to the very point of decision.

Local churches should see every gathering they have—worship service, Bible study, life group, mission project, fellowship, prayer meetings, and even business meetings—as evangelistic gatherings because they are all exercises in either the work of nudging and guiding people to where God wants them to be or the work of bringing people to the big moment of decision. We don't have to know exactly what God is calling people into to do these works. What is needed is that we learn the languages of both works and integrate that language into all of our activities.

Growing churches tend to do these works well, especially in worship services. They see every worship service as a destiny-shaping and destiny-determining opportunity, and they are relentless in inviting people to make their needed, decisive turns to God. The preaching at these churches is never treated casually but carried out with the conviction that "for at least one person listening, this sermon is your decisive call to destiny."

Given our broader understanding of evangelism, it should be obvious that evangelism is not the work of just a committee of people in our local churches, nor is it the work of organized churches alone. We are all called to pray for the Kingdom to come and be witnesses (Matthew 6:9-13; 28:16-20; Acts 1:6-8) and evangelists for God's Kingdom. So, whatever is our lot in that "location," we are to fulfill this task, and the most effective way to do that is by learning to discern and maximize Kingdom moments.

With this perspective, parents will function as "Kingdom evangelists" who look for and make the most of Kingdom moments as the way of guiding and shaping their children's lives. Parenting is a very challenging assignment. We desire things for our children that we know will increase their chances to live healthy, happy, and productive lives, but children, especially as they get older, resist their parents' influence and control. Some parents make the mistake of trying to force their opinions on their children through fear tactics or manipulation, and we end up driving our children away from us and sometimes into acts of rebellion that make their lives even more miserable. A better strategy for guiding our children is to learn to use Kingdom moments. The key is that we have to pay attention and look for those moments, especially during those times and seasons when our children don't want us to know when they are thinking deeply about their lives.

In my own life as a father and also having watched hundreds upon hundreds of kids grow up—nieces, nephews, children of friends to children in local churches—I have concluded that in the first seventeen years of children's lives, if, along with the daily guiding and shaping, we can guide children **to and in** five to seven decisive Kingdom moments, there's a strong likelihood that they will be set on the path to their purpose and destiny in the Kingdom of God. If we need five to seven Kingdom moments in seventeen years, then we have to be "plugged in" and prepared. We can't afford to miss these powerful opportunities.

Additionally, this is why we need vital and anointed ministries for children and youth in our local churches. Some of these five to seven Kingdom moments may happen while they are participating in these ministries. This is why part of the task of parenting is to provide our children with a village of people besides their parents. This is why parents must be engaged in the schools their children attend. We never know when or where our children's hearts will open to a Kingdom moment, but we should do all we can to surround them with people and resources that can help them in those moments.

We can be Kingdom evangelists in our marriages, our friendships, our professional relationships, schools, businesses, justice-advocacy organizations, and even in whole cities. We can do the work of nudging and guiding people toward their next Kingdom moment, big opportunity, or moment of transformation!

What's the real purpose of marriage? You are married to be used by God to help your spouse get to, see, and maximize his or her Kingdom moments.

Why do you have the job you have? You have the job not just to make a living but to make life by helping your coworkers get to, see, and maximize Kingdom moments.

Today, this very day, you will have opportunities to help people get to, see, or maximize a Kingdom moment. If you pay attention, you increase the likelihood that they will pay attention too, and if they catch the moment, they will walk into a Kingdom where all things are possible!

Discipleship and Training

Discipleship in faith communities and training in other types of communities is to cultivate moments, because these are the essential ways that moments get transformed into long-term movements that can make greater impact and create more deeply rooted change in us. Discipleship and training turn a coup into a new regime. In Wesleyan circles, we refer to this as *sanctifying grace.*

It is startling and unsettling to see how many followers of Jesus treat consistent Bible study, fellowship, and service as optional Christian activities. Even among church leaders, so many find greater value in a church business meeting than they find in a Bible study or participation in a service mission. When we inquire with these persons as to why they don't participate in spiritual growth activities, they usually refer to the big moment in which they submitted to God. However, as we discussed in the previous chapter, if we submit to a big moment but don't go on to total surrender, we will fail to maximize the big moment. Big moments, as wonderful as they are, can wane over time when they are not backed up with follow-through action.

Discipleship programs make us vulnerable to the Holy Spirit who can then work on us and within us, shaping us to live as Jesus did in the world.

Beyond the church setting, the same rules apply for the importance of training programs. The best marriages aren't the marriages that just had a great wedding moment but are the marriages of couples who invest time in learning how to be better spouses and how to build a stronger relationship. The best schools are those that have leaders and teachers who constantly avail themselves of the newest and best practices of grade school education. The best activist and advocacy organizations don't just wait for something bad to happen and react. They invest time and resources in training participants, at the grassroots level, on how to effectively engage in their work.

We've all heard or witnessed stories of times when a family got excited because a family member who has an apparent drug addiction finally admitted to needing help and enrolled in a recovery program. Then that family member left the rehab center after only a couple of days, the drug addiction continued, and in fact, it worsened. The person had a moment but never gave the "discipleship" program a chance to build lasting transformation.

This story is a metaphor for all of us. We will have our moments because God is good and God is coming after us with unquenchable desire for us to live the Kingdom life, the best life we can ever live.

Yet, unless we surrender to discipleship and training, we will end up as people with a thousand testimonies of miraculous deliverance without any substantive change in our lives. May this not be so with us and for us.

Final Reflection and Prayer

In 2 Kings 6:15-20, there is a powerful story of the prophet Elisha, who was with his servant inside a city, and they were surrounded by army of their enemies. Elisha's servant started to panic in fear, and Elisha said to him, "Do not be afraid, for there are more with us than there are with them." The servant continued to fret, however, because he couldn't see that there was an army of angels protecting him and Elisha. So, Elisha prayed to the Lord to open his servant's eyes. When he opened his eyes, the servant saw "the mountain was full of horses and chariots of fire."

Sometimes, we simply can't see what God is doing all around us. My prayer is that God will not only continue to send us Kingdom moments but also open our eyes that we will see them.

God, thank you for giving us Kingdom moments, gateways into your Kingdom. Open our eyes to see more of these moments. As you give us more moments, give us also the grace we need to embrace them, submit to them, and surrender to them. Keep us in a place of surrender until our big moments become sustained movements toward and within your Kingdom. May our moments turn into movements that become living monuments of Your Kingdom, Your Love, Your Power, and Your glory. In the name of Jesus, Your Son, and the Kingdom bringer, we ask these things. Amen.

Reflection Questions

This section of the book includes questions that can aid you in igniting, seeing, and/or maximizing Kingdom moments. You are encouraged to spend significant time reflecting on and discussing each question. Your goal is not to complete the list of questions as quickly as possible but to explore the potential for a Kingdom experience that's buried in each question.

Questions for Couples

1. Can you describe how you want your relationship to be in 5 years?

2. If God revealed to the two of you that today is the last day on earth for one of you, what would you say to each other?

3. What's the most important thing about you that you've never revealed to your spouse/mate?

4. If you could take back any one moment that has happened in your relationship, what would it be and why?

5. Who's the one person who has been the greatest blessing to your relationship?

6. What's the best gift your mate has ever given you?

7. Is there a song, poem, or piece of art that depicts your relationship?

8. What's the best gift you've given to the world together?

9. What's the one thing you ask God most often to do for your mate?

10. What is God saying to the world through your mate?

Questions for Families

1. What's absolutely bound to happen when we all come together?

2. Who's the rock of our family? (Or who are the pillars of our family?)

3. When are you at your best as a family?

4. What are our family's unspoken but well-known truths?

5. What's the weakness of our family?

6. What are the untapped resources of our family?

7. What do we fear most as a family, and what are we doing about it?

8. Which family member(s) have we neglected?

9. What's the funniest thing that's ever happened in/with your family?

10. What is God's message to the world through your family?

Questions for Churches

1. What's the best thing about your church?

2. When was the last time your church experienced or witnessed a miracle? What was it?

3. What kinds of people make you feel uncomfortable?

4. Who are the people in your church who tend to get neglected or overlooked?

5. Who are the people in your surrounding community who are neglected or overlooked?

6. What does your church fight about the most?

7. Can you describe how you want your church to be in five years?

8. Does your church need to apologize to the community and make amends for anything?

9. What are your church's secrets?

10. What's one thing you could do now that could make life better for people in your surrounding community and city?

Questions for Friends

1. What's the one thing that most brings the two of you together?

2. What's the untouchable subject in your friendship?

3. When did you stay mad at each other for an extended period? Why? What brought you back together?

4. How are you different from each other?

5. Do you compete? In what ways?

6. What's the weakness of your friendship?

7. Who or what are enemies of your friendship?

8. For what have you not forgiven each other?

9. What was your greatest shared adventure?

10. What is God saying to the world through your friendship?

Questions for Parents

1. What was the first thing you thought when you learned you were expecting your children?

2. What is your child or children great at doing?

3. What spiritual gifts do you see in your child and how early did you notice them?

4. What are your child's biggest fears?

5. What are your child's deepest desires and dreams?

6. What's your child's deepest wound?

7. What makes your child laugh hard and out loud?

8. What darkness does your child know about you that hasn't been spoken?

9. For what do you need to ask your child to forgive you?

10. What do you think is your child's divine purpose?

Questions for Businesses

1. Why was this business started?

2. What is our true economic engine?

3. What's the strength of this organization?

4. What Kingdom missions are impacted by your organization?

5. How does your organization handle underperforming employees?

6. How does your organization handle employees who are great producers but have negative attitudes or abusive behavior?

7. Who or what are the sacred cows of your organization?

8. What are the unspoken truths in your organization—those things that, if they were acknowledged, your organization could potentially improve?

9. What social or communal evils does your organization commit, support, or condone that it needs to oppose?

10. What sacrifices can your organization make for the public good?

Questions for Justice Organizations

1. How does your organization define and measure justice?

2. Does your organization practice justice internally?

3. What kinds of people does your organization struggle to embrace or show kindness toward?

4. Does your organization pray for God's guidance before determining specific initiatives for a particular place and time?

5. Does your organization practice internal, financial integrity? Are your financial decisions consistent with your commitment to justice?

6. What are the things your organization will fight for, even if you know you probably will not win the fight?

7. Who or what is your organization's greatest opposition?

8. Does your organization engage in justice work when there's no publicity or public awareness of your work?

9. What's your organization's greatest accomplishment?

10. Who would be negatively impacted the most if your organization fails to meet its objectives this year?

Questions for Individuals

1. What makes you come alive?

2. What makes you fiercely angry?

3. What breaks your heart?

4. What is your greatest desire for yourself, your family, your church, your community, your city, and the world?

5. How does God tend to use you to be a blessing to others?

6. What are your deepest secrets?

7. What things do you avoid in life?

8. What shortcuts do you tend to take in life?

9. Who hurt you the most?

10. What's the one thing you hope people will see or know about you when you die?

Notes

Chapter 1

1   Martin Luther King Jr., quoted in Jonathan Eig, *King: A Life* (New York: Farrar, Straus, and Giroux, 2023), chaps. 13–14, Kindle.

2   See Robert Glenn Johnson, *Jesus Unchained : How to Rise Above the Agendas, Find Peace, and Be Set Free* (Plano, TX: Invite Press, 2022), 126–29.

3   Benjamin E. Mayes, "I Have Only Just a Minute," https://prufrocksdilemma.wordpress.com/2020/08/15/i-have-only-just-a-minute/.

Chapter 2

1   Sue Bender, *Plain and Simple: A Woman's Journey to the Amish* (San Francisco: HarperSanFrancisco, 1989), 149.

Chapter 3

1   Elizabeth Barrett Browning, *Aurora Leigh* (Oxford: Oxford University Press, 1993).

Chapter 4

1   Robert Glenn Johnson, *Jesus Unchained* (Plano, TX: Invite Press, 2022), 120–48.

Chapter 5

1   David M. Shaw, "Restoring a Hemorrhaged Identity: The Identity and Impact of the Bleeding Woman in Luke 8:40–56, *Bulletin for Biblical Research* 30, no. 1 (April 17, 2020): https://doi.org/10.5325/bullbiblrese.30.1.0064.

2   Fresh Expressions United Methodist, accessed September 28, 2023, https://www.umcdiscipleship.org/equipping-leaders/fresh-expressions.

3   M. Scott Peck, *The Road Less Traveled: A New Psychology of Love, Traditional Values and Spiritual Growth*, 25th anniversary ed. (New York: Touchstone, 2012), 15–17.

4   Colin Powell , with Joseph E. Persico, *My American Journey* (New York: Ballantine, 1995), 52.

5   Heart.com.uk, "10 Stars Who Were Rejected Before Making It Big," Heart, accessed September 28, 2023, https://www.heart.co.uk/showbiz/10-stars-who-were-rejected-before-making-it-big/oprah-winfrey.

6   Ernest Hemingway, *A Farewell to Arms* (New York: Scribner, 1995), 249.

7   Derek Amato, *My Beautiful Disaster : My Brain Injury, My Gift, My Life* (Morrisville, NC: Lulu.com, 2013).

Chapter 6

1   Nadine Stair, "If I Had My Life to Live over Again," Free Your Mind, October 22, 2014, https://free-yourmind.com/2014/10/if-i-had-my-life-to-live-over-by-nadine-stair-age-85/.

Chapter 7

1   Rabbi Lawrence Kushner, *Jewish Spirituality: A Brief Introduction for Christians* (Woodstock, NY: Jewish Lights, 2001), 24–25.

2   See "Eric Thomas Be Phenomenal or Be Forgotten Motivational Speech," YME DUO TV, May 13, 2014, YouTube video, https://www.youtube.com/watch?v=6N1OmEOM3LE.

SCAN HERE to learn more about Invite Press, a premier publishing imprint created to invite people to a deeper faith and living relationship with Jesus Christ.